Hello, Refugees!

Tuvia Tenenbom

The Jewish Theater of New York Incorporated

New York, NY

Hello, Refugees!
Tuvia Tenenbom

Photos, design & proofreading:
Isi Tenenbom

Cover:
Shay Charka

Inquiries:
NewYorkPress@me.com

Published in association with
The Jewish Theater of New York

Printed in the United States of America

ISBN 978-0-9839399-4-8

Critics Praise **Hello, Refugees!**

(For the German edition, *Allein unter Flüchtlingen*)

A piercing storyteller whose writing is full of humor and irony.
Frankfurter Allgemeine Zeitung

His reportage is precisely the right antidote we need: fearless and open-minded.
Badische Zeitung

Tenenbom is the Michael Moore of nonfiction.
Bayrischer Rundfunk

Relentlessly honest.
Mitteldeutsche Zeitung

Clever.
Cicero

Tenenbom's polemical writing causes people to argue, and this is good.
Der Tagesspiegel

This book is full of uncomfortable truths; probably one of the most valuable guides for those who are planning to participate in the upcoming general election.
Jüdische Rundschau

Entertaining, humorous, whimsical, critical and provocative.
SWR2

Hello, Refugees! is not about hard figures, but about impressions and actual stories that we would never be aware of them had Tuvia Tenenbom not written this book.
General-Anzeiger

International Praise for Tuvia Tenenbom's Previous Work

Highly engaging and emotional, eminently readable, brutally honest.
Publishers Weekly

Irresistibly fascinating...seductive and engaging.
New York Times

Illuminating and alarming.
Wall Street Journal

The Lies They Tell ranks Tenenbom among the best social anthropologists, like Comte Alexis de Tocqueville and Mark Twain.
American Thinker

Read what Tenenbom has to tell us, without bias. We don't have the privilege not to know.
Haaretz (Israel)

Tenenbom's laughter touches our soul in places where mere intellect could never reach.
Die Zeit (Germany)

One of the most iconoclastic and innovative of contemporary dramatists.
Corriere Della Sera (Italy)

A daring and hilariously written account.
Commentary

Tuvia Tenenbom is Michael Moore and *Borat* in one.
Die Welt (Germany)

A force of nature . . . provocative, satirical, intellectual.
La Repubblica (Italy)

A free artist who fights for truth and tolerance.
Le Vif L Express (Belgium)

A mystical provocateur.
Le Monde (France)

Brilliant.
Deutschlandradio (Germany)

Tuvia is curious as a cat, sly as a fox, friendly as a Labrador, and is also a man with seismographic sensitivities.
Mida (Israel)

Tenenbom rides the razor's edge...and goes all the way off.
Amsterdam News

Amazingly original.
Jewish Currents

Fresh and audacious.
Village Voice

Hugely entertaining, terribly funny, sarcastic, engaging, powerful, accusatory, judgmental, good!
National Review

Here is a man, a writer, who does not follow patterns of thought dictated by others, nor does he abide by a code of language that others have imposed. And yet, he keeps his sense of humor throughout the pages.
Spiegel Online (Germany)

• • •

TUVIA TENENBOM, a three-in-a-row *Spiegel* bestselling author and a recent recipient of the Honest Journalism Award in Berlin, is a journalist and dramatist. He holds advanced degrees in both fine arts and science, and is the founder of the Jewish Theater of New York.

Tuvia's articles and essays have been published in leading Western media including Germany's *Die Zeit, Focus* and *Die Welt*; Italy's *Corriere della Sera*; Israel's *Yedioth Ahronoth, Makor Rishon* and the *Jerusalem Post*; and Fox News and the *Forward*. His previous books include the international bestsellers *The Lies They Tell, Catch the Jew!* and *I Sleep in Hitler's Room.*

To Isi,
Whose presence and dedication made the journey
worthwhile at every turn

CONTENTS

Thanks & Acknowledgements

I am grateful to the sons and daughters of the Levant in Germany who have asked me to serve as their mouthpiece, am indebted to migrants of countries large and small who have shared their stories with me, am thankful to the German people who have allowed me an opening into their deeper selves, and am beholden to politicians and lawmakers for introducing me to their outer selves. My apologies, may I add here, go to camp security personnel for breaking their rules at every possible turn.

I owe a debt of gratitude to Jonathan Landgrebe and Winfried Hörning for trusting me with this project and making this book available to the reading public.

My thanks to Florian Krauss and Daniel Till for engraving this journey for posterity in digital form, and to Lori Lowenthal Marcus for going over the manuscript and graciously sharing her comments and corrections with me.

Warmest thanks to my mother-in-law, Isa Lowy, for the care and love she has shown to me ever since we first met.

Commissioned by the Suhrkamp publishing company in Berlin, this book was published in German by Suhrkamp earlier this year under the title *Allein unter Flüchtlingen*.

Chapter 1

Germany: Refugee Nation

Syria, or whatever is left of it, is around the corner from me, but I can't go there. I am, lo and behold, in Syria's biggest enemy state: Israel. I mean, that's the way things used to be. Today nobody knows who Syria's biggest enemy is, least of all the Syrians or the Israelis. Sometimes I walk around the streets of Israel and tell people that I'm Syrian. When I do this, the Jews ask me if I'm Christian and the Arabs ask me if I'm Muslim. Why do I pretend to be Syrian? I don't know. I have been to the Arab world more than once, in Saudi Arabia, Jordan, Qatar, and Egypt, but never to Syria. I met some Syrians here and there, and I loved them, don't ask me why – love is hard to explain. I like the Arab world in general, but I have a 'thing' for the Syrians.

How many Syrians are walking the streets of Israel these days? I'm not sure but probably somewhere between zero and two, take or leave a couple here or there.

Yes, there are a few Syrians in this country, since Israel has accepted some of the wounded in the Syrian civil war for treatment at its hospitals, but none of those Syrians are walking; they are lying.

Where are the walking Syrians? Rumor has it that many of them, hundreds of thousands of them, are in Germany – and more of them could be coming still.

Germany, that's where I could mingle with Syrians. With all kinds of them, by the way. A German friend, hear this, just sent me a copy of an invite to an event in Germany that will feature "panel discussion with and about queer refugees." The event is organized by no less than the Green Party, I read in the invite. Wow! This is something that a man like me can not miss. I don't know if I should go public with it but, between you and me, it has always been a secret dream of mine to mingle with Syrian lesbians and transgender Afghanis. And after receiving this invite, it seems to me that the Green Party's event is the perfect opportunity to make my dream come true. It will be awesome, I'm sure. I've never met a Queer Muslim in my life, but if I fly to Germany I'll be surrounded by them!

I promptly reserve a plane ticket, getting mentally ready to fly out of the Holy Land and into the land of the Germans.

Granted, this is not the only reason why I'll be flying to Germany. I have been commissioned by my publisher, Suhrkamp, to write a book about the refugee issue in Germany, but I've been postponing my flight to Germany because where I am, may I tell you, the food is extraordinarily delicious.

I'm doing very well here, in case you wondered. I rented a flat right in the middle of a huge market in Jerusalem, the Mahane Yehuda market, and I'm having a blast. The market, teeming with people, is open twenty hours a day and the food here was cooked in Paradise, though they charge very little for it. To put it mildly, this is Heaven. But, I must add, no one here, at least as far as I know, is a transgender Muslim. This kind of people, I guess, feel happiest in Berlin.

I take a break from the food and go to feed my curiosity.

I fly to Germany.

Sitting in the plane, I try to collect my thoughts about the whole refugee issue. What do I know about the refugees in Germany, or outside of it? I ask myself.

Hello, Refugees!

Not much. I read about this issue in the media, mostly American and British, but that's about it. I read, for example, that Turkey hosts the highest number of refugees, totaling over 2.5 million; that Lebanon and Jordan host around two million between the two of them, but that most other Arab countries have not accepted any meaningful number of refugees, if at all; that in 2015 Germany took in 1.1 million refugees from Syria, Afghanistan, and other nations, and that no other European country has accepted as many refugees as Germany. In the *New York Times*, America's power paper, there was an Op-Ed article the other day titled: "Germany, Refugee Nation." Not bad, huh?

I'm thirsty. I need a drink, but the plane's crew doesn't serve drinks yet. Hopefully, in a few minutes the drink carts will start rolling in the cabin. I should have bought a bottle of Diet Coke, my favorite drink, before mounting the plane but I was too late to do it. I was standing outside smoking my Indonesian cigarettes, the best cigarettes in the world, and had to rush to the gate just before it had closed.

What else do I know about the refugee issue?

In mid-July of 2015, there was a televised event that showed the German Chancellor Angela Merkel in an exchange with a fourteen-year-old Palestinian girl from Lebanon. The girl said to Angela, internationally known as "Mama," that she was afraid of being deported back to Lebanon, and Angela replied that there was nothing much she could do for her. I have the exact exchange on my iPad. Can you believe it? "You know," Angela said to the girl, "there are thousands and thousands in the Palestinian refugee camps in Lebanon, and if we say 'you can all come,' and 'you can all come from Africa,' we cannot handle that." The young girl burst into tears and Angela walked over to her, in an attempt to comfort her, but the way Angela did it was quite awkward, and Angela's image as a "Mama" was a bit damaged.

And soon enough, Angela had a change of heart and Germany was taking in more and more refugees. "Wir schaffen das," "We can do it," Mama said at a press conference in late August. She probably learned this sound bite from the American

3

president, Barack Obama, whose first election slogan was, "Yes We Can."

In early September, when Hungary blocked refugees from crossing through its territory and used tear gas to push them away, Angela decided to forgo Europe's Dublin Regulation and allowed the refugees to come to Germany from Hungary. Dublin Regulation states that asylum seekers must request asylum in the country they first arrive, but Angela apparently didn't care much about such rules. To her, and to many Germans – especially of the cultural elite – the rule that they must stick by is Germany's Basic Law, Article 16a, paragraph 1, which states: "Persons persecuted on political grounds shall have the right of asylum."

Period.

The truth is that paragraph 2 of this Article states: "Paragraph (1) of this Article may not be invoked by a person who enters the federal territory from a member state of the European Communities." But so what? Like any law in the world, this one can be interpreted in many ways, and Mama knows best.

I cull this information, by the way, from my iPad. Part of my brain, if you care to know, is inside this iPad. Yeah, really. If I lose this iPad, I'll lose half of my IQ; I'm not kidding.

When are they coming with the drinks? I need a Diet Coke. Now. I hope they don't charge for it. You never know airlines; soon they will charge for your seat and for toilet use. Yes, yes, you'll see. In ten or twenty years every commercial aircraft will have a standing room section, and there will be different toilet sizes, depending on how much you'll be willing to pay. It's coming, baby; Western capitalism knows no borders.

What else is on my iPad? Well, here goes: On September 11 the *Deutsche Welle* quoted Angela Merkel thusly: "The fundamental right to asylum for the politically persecuted knows no upper limit; that also goes for refugees who come to us from the hell of a civil war." When the Syrians heard this, they flocked to Germany. Wouldn't you? If what I read elsewhere on my iPad is correct, Germany will gladly accept hundreds of thousands of refugees in each of the coming years. This is the time to get a German passport, my dear, if you ever wanted one.

Only that Mama, pretty quickly, had a change of heart again. On September 13, the *Guardian* wrote that "Germany introduced border controls on Sunday, and dramatically halted all train traffic with Austria after the country's regions said they could no longer cope with the overwhelming number of refugees entering the country."

About a month later, I see on my iPad, the British *Independent* wrote that Angela Merkel "held talks with Turkey's President Recep Tayyip Erdogan and his Prime Minister Ahmet Davutoglu in the hope of securing Ankara's help in reinforcing a buffer zone in the region to slow the tide of war refugees from Syria and Afghanistan currently entering Europe."

Day followed day, week followed week, month followed month, and before anybody realized it, the year 2015 was gone and 2016 showed up and with it the Sylvester celebration -- what in America you'd call the New Year's Eve celebration.

I think, though I'm not sure, that the flight attendants are getting ready to offer drinks to the passengers. It's time!

When the clock strikes 12 in Times Square, New York City, tens of thousands of people exchange kisses with their beloveds. But Germany is not the USA, and on Sylvester 2016 quite some people did something entirely different than exchanging kisses. To be specific, they raped. It happened in some cities in Germany, but nowhere else was it as acute as in Cologne. Thousands of men, who according to eyewitnesses looked "Arabic" or "North African," congregated in the plaza between the central train station and the famous Cologne Cathedral and many of them started "playing" with German women. Groping here, stealing there, inserting fingers in vaginas here and squeezing breasts there, beating up women here and raping others there – until they had enough. In the days and weeks that followed, over a thousand complaints were filed with the police.

I was in New York when this happened, and I remember that this story came to my attention not from the media but from the social media. The mainstream media, it turned out days later, knew what was happening in the plaza and nearby streets but chose not to share what they knew with the public. Why? If the people knew, they said to themselves, they would get angry with Angela's "open door" policy for the refugees, and in the next election they would vote for the far-right party, Alternative for Germany (Alternative für Deutschland), known by its initials AfD.

Personally, I'm part of the German media, having a column about politics in *Zeit Online*, and I know how the German media operate. Most German journalists that I've come across believe that journalism is an "educational" tool, where facts matter much less than "proper thinking." They view themselves a cut above the "masses," and they think that it's their obligation to make the people think properly, which in this case meant that the people should stick with Mama.

But what does Mama think?

It's hard to know.

In March of 2016, the European Union, via Angela, reached a complicated deal with Turkey. Under the terms of the deal Turkey will tighten its borders to prevent refugees from crossing into Greece; refugees who cross from Turkey into Greece will be sent back to Turkey; for every Syrian being shipped to Turkey, the EU will accept one Syrian already in Turkey, up to 72,000 Syrians; refugees who are legally admissible in the EU, and ask for asylum, will be allowed to stay; Turkey will get six billion euros and some other goodies

In short, to sum this deal up in one sentence: Germany will still be seen as accepting refugees, only the refugees won't arrive in Germany because they will be stuck somewhere far away, dead or alive.

I laugh to myself quietly when I recall the title of an op-ed in the *New York Times*: "Germany, Refugee Nation."

Laugh or not, flying on this German plane is no laughing matter. The seat is narrow, not just for a fat man like me. The distance between the rows is most likely forbidden by many religions, but airlines are notorious atheists. If you are not extra careful, you are doomed to continually push against the person in front of you with your knees. Catholic priests, I believe, will get a kick of it but I'm not Catholic, at least not yet.

And there are no drinks yet!

When will this flight end, oh God?

There should be, I think, a Geneva Convention on Fliers which would grant airline customers fundamental rights, such as minimum legroom. There's a Geneva Convention on Refugees, by the way. That Convention is grounded in support of Article 14 of the Universal Declaration of Human Rights, which states that "everyone has the right to seek and to enjoy in other countries asylum from persecution." The Geneva Convention on Fliers would state: "Everyone has the right to enjoy their flight and have the capacity to move their legs in a comfortable, natural and human manner."

Convention or not, time moves on and I finally get a lukewarm Diet Coke, which is horrible. I have no idea how people, almost always non-Americans, drink lukewarm Diet Coke.

To make a long story short, the plane lands.

No, not in Berlin; not yet. I'm stretching my legs in Hamburg.

Why Hamburg?

You see, some Germans have told me – Germans, if you didn't know, are often in need to share refugee stories with strangers – that if I wanted I could see refugees living in one of Hamburg's nicer quarters, the villa-lined neighborhood of Harvestehude.

Before I meet queer refugees, I should meet wealthy refugees.

Good thinking, isn't it?

Well, I think so.

In any case, I arrive at the neighborhood of villas before sunset.

Chapter 2

Germans Don't Kill People. Period.

The Harvestehude neighborhood, let me tell you, is gorgeous. If I ever get to be a German Chancellor, which is my next mission in life, I think I'd buy a villa here. But if the Chancellorship dream does not materialize, for whatever reason, I will take a flight to Syria and return to Germany as a refugee.

It's a lovely place, this neighborhood, and quite picturesque.

I enjoy the sights unfolding in front of my eyes, of beautiful villas that beg me to own them. Right ahead of me, as I walk, is something that looks like a gallery, where all kinds of Buddhist sculptures decorate an opulent property. Look: Here's Buddha, next to an inspiring tree, surrounded by artsy lighting.

Lovely Buddha.

Remember when the Germans were into Buddha? I do. That was a fun period in German history, my German history.

When I first came to Germany from the United States, about a decade and a half ago, every third German I met was into Buddha.

That was a lovely time! I couldn't stop listening to my new German friends, especially when they were sitting on the floor, eating grass, lighting candles and chatting in what they thought was Hindu. They were trying to tell me, in a thick German accent, fascinating stories about death and nirvana.

I don't meet those people anymore. The ones I knew grew older, each made a baby or three-quarters of a baby, got divorced, and then one day disappeared from my life. God knows where they are now; maybe in New Delhi.

I leave Buddha behind and keep on walking. And then, standing near magnificent villas on a street called Sophienterrassen, I spot ahead of me a building which is not exactly a villa. The building, built by people of no imagination, used to be an administrative building of some kind, I find out. The city of Hamburg, I'm told, invested close to twenty million euros in buying this property and converted it into a home for about two hundred refugees.

I go there, and I walk in.

The place is packed with refugees of all kinds and sorts, adults and children, and I make my acquaintance with a lovely Arab couple. He is Lebanese, and she is originally from Syria, but both lived in Lebanon before they arrived here.

How did you get to Germany? I ask them, anticipating a touching story of people fighting the elements on an inflated boat about to capsize at any second but the couple's spirit, stronger than the roughest wind and the toughest of waves, lifts them up and sends them directly to Germany. You know, the kind of stories I read in the papers. But no. They did not challenge the elements to get here. They made their way to Germany, they tell me, in the easiest way possible, on a plane, arriving here together with their two sons.

The man, who used to be a clothes salesman, is busy these days studying German because he was led to understand by the powers that be that if he didn't study German, he would get less money from the German government. His wife doesn't study anything; she claims that she's sick and that she can't possibly sit, only lie, and therefore cannot attend any class. That's okay with the Germans, who are friendly people, and they won't reduce a penny out of what they pay her.

I enter their room.

She sits now; I'm no German teacher, and so that's good.

The man looks at me, immediately calculating that I need something in my mouth. Would you like coffee? he asks.

Of course, I do.

He prepares the coffee for me, Arabic coffee.

Oh, Allah! I drink this coffee, and I want to convert to Islam right away!

I sip more and more of the black magic while listening to the wife who is telling me that back there in the Middle East she converted to Christianity some years ago and that's why they had to leave Lebanon. In Lebanon, according to her, those who have converted out of Islam face the threat of death every day because Muslims have a peculiar aversion to people who leave the faith.

Was she threatened by anyone? Allah knows.

I keep sipping the magic concoction.

And after a few more sips, she tells me that Germany is a great place.

Her husband concurs.

How so?

Germany is a rich country, they both say, and the "Germans love us."

Why do they love you? What do you think?

They have no answer. Instead, they tell me that each member of their family, each of the four of them, gets four hundred euros a month, a gift of the German people.

Their housing is free, food is free, but there's no alcohol.

Well, with €1,600 they can, if they so wish, buy a bottle or three.

The man, by the way, is a massage therapist as well and he treats me, for two minutes, for free.

I get another cup of coffee, and I'm in heaven.

"In Syria, people kill each other, slaughter each other, but in Germany people are nice, very nice. The Germans are civilized people; they don't kill," the wife says.

Don't kill?

"No! The Germans are nice!"

The coffee is great, I tell them.

"You want more? We have more!"

Thank you, thank you. By the way: Do you know what happened here, in beautiful Hamburg, seventy or eighty years ago? Do you know what the Germans did?

They stare at me. Both man and woman, who answer to the names Tanios and Maha, are now silent. I bid them goodbye, and I walk out.

They were my first refugees on this journey. Will the others be like them?

On the next day, I take a train to Berlin. Got to meet other refugees, the Syrian Queers.

Chapter 3

Queer Muslims Mingle with German Politicians

I like trains, especially German trains. They are fast, they are clean, and they are on time.

Many Germans don't like when I say this. The trains are never on time, they complain. Are they right? For the most part, they are not, but they like to kvetch.

Germans love to kvetch, just like Jews. I've learned this long ago.

The train ride to Berlin is smooth, much better than the average American train, and is quite fast.

An impeccably-dressed lady, an employee of the train company, walks around with a tray of coffees. Would you like coffee? she asks. Well, why not? I buy a cup of cappuccino. The coffee, quite costly, comes in a small paper cup. Near the top of the cup is a little line with the number 0.3, meaning 0.3 liters. When I lift the cover, I see that the foam reaches exactly the 0.3 mark. That's Germany. Exact.

Yesterday the Lebanese gave me coffee in a glass, not in a paper cup, and there were no lines on it. Who needs lines? Nobody in Lebanon has any use for such lines. But we are not in Lebanon. Here it's Germany, this is a train, and the coffee cups have marks and lines on them.

What can I tell you? The Arabic coffee, the one in the glass with no marks, was much, much, much better than this coffee.

I can't finish the lousy 0.3 cup, sorry for kvetching, and soon enough the train reaches Berlin. I get off and move on to the Party.

Posters and brochures carrying the slogan, "Du. Wir. Queer" ("You. We. Queer") greet the people who come in, and once the people are inside, they get busy drinking alcoholic beverages. Are they Muslims? I thought that Muslims don't drink alcohol, but maybe Queer Muslims do.

Hello, Refugees!

Wait a second! These people don't look Arabic or Afghani, Persian or Pakistani! They are as Muslim as much as I am Syrian. They are German! Where are the Syrian queers? Where are the Afghani transgender? I can't find them. I look around me, at this queer event, and the faces staring back at me are Germanic. Could it be that Syrian, or Afghani, queers are by nature similar to Germans in appearance?

Yes, could be.

Everything is possible in Germany, I learned along the years. The strangest things are happening in Germany; that's the history of this place.

Whoever these people are, drinks are not the only thing offered here. This a political party, after all, and politicians are into speeches, which is exactly what takes place at this very moment. The speakers, by the way, deliver their speeches in perfect German, with no foreign accent to speak of.

I meet Volker Beck, a member of the Bundestag and the spokesperson for migration and religious policies of the Green Party parliamentary faction in the Bundestag. The man has almost no hair on his head, but he looks cool nevertheless.

Hello, Refugees!

I ask him if he knows any Arab queer in the crowd, which I estimate is between two to three hundred people, and he points to one Arab queer in attendance. One.

Toni Hofreiter, a leader of the Green Party in the Bundestag, has long hair and a beard as well. He drinks beer and I go to him, asking if he knows of any Syrian queers here, and he suggests that I ask Volker.

As far as I can tell there are more Syrian Queers in Mama's bedroom than there are here. This party, I start suspecting, is just another Green Party event where the Refugee Queers idea served as a clever bait to get you and me to show up.

Not bad.

The speakers here do what speakers do everywhere: give speeches. What are they talking about? Something along the lines of having the right to marry and be merry. Nothing earth-shattering to anyone living in New York, like yours truly. But then something nice happens: a man by the name of Mahmud comes to the stage. Mahmud is a 41-year-old Syrian author, and he is a consultant for gay and lesbians in Berlin.

Mahmud is not really a refugee, but he looks like one. He left Syria for Turkey in 2011, where he worked as a journalist, and at some point was invited to Germany. He came to this land, overstayed his visa, and now he is a legal resident.

He talks about honor killings in the Kurdish areas, and of gay killings in Syria. His speech gives the impression that the only murders happening in Syria are of virgin women who have sex with men, and of men who sleep with other men. You got to be a total dumb to buy this, but with enough alcohol in your system you'll buy the Brooklyn Bridge.

Volker, as you might have expected, also speaks here. I don't pay much attention, but if I'm not wrong, he talks about gay, lesbian and transgender refugees. I wonder how many Muslims in Syria, Libya, Afghanistan, and Iraq are busy these days having sex-change operations, but everything is possible when rockets and bullets fly above your head.

When the event is over, I meet Inana, a young lady who says that she is from Syria. Dressed in short clothes, and showing flesh to all who want to see, she speaks fluent English and loves to use the word "fuck" every three seconds on average. And, oh yes, she is lesbian.

Two LGBT "refugees" at this event. That's it. Don't you love politicians? I do.

I leave the party. Let them fool each other and enjoy it.

Outside the building I meet two people, who both claim to be journalists, and one of them tells me that the AfD had just hired a Jewish lawyer to help get Angela Merkel out of office. Why would a "Jewish" lawyer do that? Because, he says, the Jewish lawyer regards Angela Merkel as a traitor.

I'm hardly one day in Germany and I already hear "Jewish lawyer" tales.

Why am I surprised?

Be it as it may, millions of people in Germany would love to see the AfD disappear from the face of the earth, but there are quite many others who like them and they rise in the polls.

Led by the energetic Frauke Petry, AfD is an upstart right-wing political party known for its "anti-Muslim" philosophy. In May of 2016, the AfD adopted a manifesto which called to ban minarets in mosques, as well as the wearing of burkas by women. The Muslims of Germany, of course, don't like the AfD one bit. In fact, Aiman Mazyek, the head of the Central Council of Muslims in Germany, compared the ideology of the AfD to that of Hitler's Nazi Party.

I think, though I can't guarantee it, that the AfD has no party tonight starring Syrian Queers and Afghani transgender. What a shame!

I take a taxi to my hotel and chat a bit with the driver, a guy who likes to talk. He shares with me, for example, that journalists collect their information by speaking with taxi drivers and then go to their offices and write what they heard the "people" say. That's not fair, he says, because there are much more people in the world than just taxi drivers.

What do the German journalists ask you most these days?

"They want to know my opinion about refugees."

His observation about journalists, I'd say, is correct.

Get your ass out of this cab and go meet refugees, I say to myself. But where do the refugees live, other than in Harvestehude?

I'll have to find out.

Chapter 4

Would You Like to Have Sex in a Refugee Camp?

If you wanted to reach the capital of Germany on a plane years ago, when the world was less advanced, and air passengers enjoyed excellent legroom, you would have probably found yourself landing at Tempelhof Airport, Germany's legendary airport at the time.

At some point in history, which Tanios and Maha prefer not to remember, Tempelhof, an area in the center of Berlin, hosted a Nazi concentration camp. In the same area there was also a forced labor camp, where poor souls toiled from dawn to dust at the Tempelhof Airport until the end of the Second World War. But Tempelhof Airport did not serve only the Nazis; it served the Allies as well. In the late forties of the last century Allied aircraft, known to locals as the Raisin Bombers, scattered raisins and chocolates over Berlin during the Berlin Airlift, an operation that saved West Berlin from falling into the hands of the Soviets.

History, this is what Berlin is really about. Isn't it?

Earlier this year a new chapter of history was written in Berlin: the opening of the Tempelhof Refugee Center, designed to hold up to seven thousand refugees, turning the Tempelhof's old airport into Germany's largest refugee center.

So I am told.

Got to see this one.

How will I get there?

A taxi.

Driven by a Turkish guy, who lives in this country for over two decades and loves Mr. Erdogan, the taxi drops me in front of a gigantic structure, reminiscent of the good, old Nazi architecture. The place is huge, but outside you can hardly see a soul. There could be thousands of people inside, but I see no one outside.

Could it be that the Erdogan lover dropped me in the wrong place?

17

I make my way to the camp, or whatever it is, in an attempt to enter the massive structure.

Should be an easy task, but it's not. And I realize this the closer I get to the place. There are guards in front of the structure, and they don't look like a happy bunch.

Yep, this is a camp. A refugee camp.

Here is a guard, with a Nike baseball cap on his head, and he tells me that I can't go in. Period. I say to him that I got some friends inside waiting for me and he asks me for their names. Mohammad Amadi, I say. Do I know Mohammad Amadi? No, but it sounds cool, doesn't it? The guard, who tells me that he hails from Cleveland, Ohio, says he doesn't know of any Mohammad Amadi inside. He suggests I contact this Amadi by phone and have him come out here to pick me up. If that Amadi materializes, he says, I would be able to enter with him. Not too deep inside, but to a guest area in Hangar 3.

The problem is that I don't know any Amadi either. I know Erdogan more than I know Amadi. How do I proceed from here?

Who else, but Lady Luck, comes to my aid. Two men, one with a cross tattooed on his neck, are approaching the airport. They seem to be refugees, and they are probably about to enter the place. They look better than any "Amadi," I say to myself. The best thing about them is that unlike Amadi they exist, they are here, in the flesh. Maybe, if they are indeed refugees, I could convince them to become my friends, and they would invite me in.

Genius plan, isn't it?

I greet them in Arabic, and they understand me. Yes, they are refugees! We start talking. They are both from Syria, they tell me.

Perfect!

Can I visit you inside? I ask them.

They don't know what the heck I want from their lives, and so I explain. I want to go inside, I share with them, but that American from Cleveland wouldn't let me in unless a resident invited me. Would you mind to be my friends for a day and host me?

In the West, where we now are, if a man you don't know approaches you with a request to become an instant friend, you would either call the police or give him ten cents, assumimg that he must be a retarded drunk on his way to a Syrian Queer Party. But the guys in front of me are not German or American; they are Syrian, my kind of people, the people I had to fly thousands of miles to meet, even though they live right next door to where I was just days ago.

Will my little trick work? It takes some convincing to do, of about a minute or a fraction thereof, and they "finally" agree to be my hosts and my friends. Yes: They are Syrian, not American and not German.

Who am I? I am a Jew, born in Israel but residing in both the United States and Germany. But this is not what I tell them. It's too much information to digest too fast. Instead, I tell them that I'm half Jordanian. More exactly: I tell them that I am half Jordanian and half German. My father is from Berlin and my mother from Amman. Today, unlike a couple of days ago, I can't be Syrian. There's no way under the sun that I could convince these Syrians that I am their lost Syrian brother.

By the way, what the heck is that American doing here?

I don't know, and I don't ask; he is a guard here, and I don't need him as my enemy.

The three of us, two Syrians and one-half Jordanian, approach the Ohioan. We tell him that we are friends from back then, and he demands my ID, which he keeps with him. In return, he gives me a little paper which is to serve as my entrance ticket. I am allowed to enter Hangar 3, and 3 only, he says.

In Hangar 3 there's something like a guest room, so to speak, with a sitting area and a table in the middle.

We sit down, them and I.

Kossai, the guy with the cross on his neck, asks me if I am "press," and I answer in the positive.

You gotta know your friends, I guess.

"No pictures of me," he says.

Okay.

He takes out his smartphone, and he shows me a photo of his home across the Mediterranean. "This is a picture of my house.

Hit by a rocket. By Daesh," he says, and adds – in case I didn't get it – "ISIS." The Islamic State, known in the Arab world as Daesh, is called ISIS, IS or ISIL in the West.

He shows me pictures of Before and After, how the house looked before the explosion, awesomely beautiful, and how it looked after, a mess of stones.

After this had happened, he tells me, he decided to leave.

Where did you go?

"Turkey."

How did you get to Turkey?

"By plane. From Lebanon."

How did you get to Lebanon? Did you walk?

"No. By taxi."

Where did you go to after Turkey?

"I stayed in Turkey one month, looking for a smuggler to take me to Greece. And then I found one."

How much did he charge you for the operation?

"One thousand and sixty-five euros. To cross the sea."

The average family in Syria, he tells me, earns $40 a month at the current exchange rate. This man must be a very wealthy man, I say to myself, or a very talented thief.

Knowing that Syria was, and probably still is, one of the most bitter enemies of Israel, I ask the two of them if they came to Germany because of this country's history of wiping out millions of Jews.

No, they say.

On the contrary, Kossai tells me; he didn't want to come to Germany at all. When he arrived in Greece, he tells me, he wanted to go to Sweden, where he has some family, but this didn't work out, and he ended up in Germany. "I was forced to be here (Germany)," he says.

Who forced you to be in Germany?

"Denmark. They took my Syrian passport from me and sent me to the German police."

The reason? As he was making his way across Europe, following his arrival in Greece, he reached Austria and there he was told to go to the German police. He went to the Germans, then ran away from them, made his way to Denmark, where he was shipped back to German authorities, which is how he got to Tempelhof.

How do you spend your time here? What do you do here?

"Waiting."

For whom, Allah?

"No."

Who, then, are you waiting for?

"I want to study German, so I could go to college and finish my studies: English Literature."

He gives me the names of the dramatists he loves: "Shakespeare, Hamlet, George Bernard Shaw."

These are my Syrians: Study German so that you could study English lit. They study English authors: Shakespeare, Hamlet, and George Bernard Shaw.

Do you think you'll stick around in Germany, get married, and—

"No. If I marry, I'll marry the one I love. She is in Syria. I want to go back after the war ends."

Do you think that the war will end?

"Yes. After ten years."

Maybe twenty, no?

"Fifteen. Twenty. I don't know."

Mohannad, his friend and now mine as well, intervenes. "The war will not finish," he says. It started by the people, who wanted to remove President Basher el-Assad from office, but now the war is controlled by a third party, not the Syrian people themselves.

Who is that third party?

"I don't know."

Are you talking about Russia, Germany…?

"Iran, Turkey, and Russia."

And the United States?

"Of course."

Israel?

"Of course. Double of course! Israel! What does Israel want? To destroy the Syrian army without shooting one bullet!"

Kossai, do you agree?

"There are fifteen countries involved in the war in Syria."

The war, Mohannad says, will not end in fifty years.

Now they are in Germany, and they will stay here for a while.

Do you like the German culture? I ask them.

Well, they prefer their own. They don't like the idea, for example, that German women "have the freedom to take off their clothes in the street; this will never happen in our country." What they don't like even more, is being here, in Tempelhof. "Here it's very bad," says Mohannad, and Kossai agrees. There are seven hangars here, they tell me, and each one of them has many "boxes," which is kind of a room, and no box has a door. There are thousands of people living here, and the sound level does not abate at any point of day or night. When people talk to each other, Kossai and Mohannad tell me, they must shout because it's so loud inside.

Can you have sex in this camp?

"No. There are two, three families in a room; no privacy."

Number of people in each box: 12. Each gets about €110 a month, "enough for my cigarettes," says Mohannad.

The food in the camp, both say, is horrible. It's supposed to be "Arabic" food, but it's not. The two commodities they do have plenty of, they share with me, are time and noise. There are German lessons, one hour a day, but they can't study anything because of the noise. There's simply no way to concentrate.

I want to see their rooms, boxes, or whatever they are called.

Kossai, who by now trusts me, is willing to show me what's inside.

My entrance ticket grants me the right to sit here, in Hangar 3, but this is just a guest room. Kossai lives in Hangar 2. We need to find a way to do this.

Kossai says: Let's try.

But how?

We come up with a plan. The guards know Kossai. and he can go anywhere; why shouldn't I just walk beside him, as if we were two Siamese cats, and "ignore" the guards.

We try it out.

The cats go to Hangar 2, which takes a couple of minutes.

When we enter the hangar, we walk "naturally," as if he is not a smuggler and I'm not an outsider.

It looks good; picture perfect. We pass the guards and are about to walk in.

Problem: one of the guards runs toward me. "Badge," he says.

No problem, I tell him and hand him over my entrance ticket.

"This is Hangar 2," he says, "and you can't go in. Only Hangar 3!"

German guards, lo and behold, are smarter than cats.

We must get out of here.

As we walk out, both of us have this one thought: How could it be that the two of us, two great Arabs, couldn't outsmart one non-Arab guard? What a shame! None of us would ever be able to look at our defeated faces in the mirror unless we do something now, something drastic that would give us back our pride, our Arabic pride.

"Let's try Hangar 1," Kossai says.

We do.

When we enter Hangar 1, a guard stops me. "Authorization to visit," he demands.

Oh, these Germans!

I need to use the toilet, I reply, and Allah has authorized this!

Kossai concurs.

The guard directs me to the guards' toilet but I am dumb, and I understand neither his English nor his German and ask Kossai to guide me. Kossai, a good pal, promptly understands that I'm probably planning something and tells the guard that I need directions, from him. The guard agrees. No German, I guess, wants to be caught preventing a retarded man like me from using the toilet.

And so Kossai comes along with me.

We reach the guards' toilet.

Kossai looks at the toilet, the simplest of toilets one could find in Germany, and he goes bananas: "Look at this! They, the guards, have such a clean and good toilet while we have the worst. I can't believe it!"

The "good" thing about this toilet, by the way, is that the floor is not dirty wet with urine and that there are functioning doors here.

Now let's walk to your hangar, I say to Kossai.

Kossai immediately agrees.

We leave the guards' toilet, walking in the direction of the hangar where the refugees live. Kossai turns on the camera of his smartphone, in selfie mode, and puts it up to see what's behind us while we are walking forward. It is on the phone that he will be able to see if any guard is following us.

Brilliant, my man!

We walk, a refugee with a smartphone and his toilet user.

Kossai, his eyes on the way ahead and on the way in the back of us, says: "They look at us, but they don't follow us. I can't believe it! It's great!"

We keep walking.

"If they stop us," says my new friend, "don't tell them you are press. They don't like journalists here!"

Got you, my man!

We keep walking, and we reach the Forbidden Hangar.

We are in.

I look at the place.

This site was designed to house planes, which means that it was never intended to serve as a housing for human beings. It's big. It's huge. And there are many "boxes" around. These boxes, rooms, cells or units – everybody around gives them another name – resemble cubicles in an American office, only that the furnishing here is of the lowest quality. There are many, many "boxes" here, one next to the other, and none has a roof or a door. In other words: no privacy at all. Each such box has bunk beds in it, beds upon beds, and there's not much else you can do in your box except for sleeping.

We reach Kossai's box.

What's inside?

Sweating people doing nothing.

It's 84 degrees (Fahrenheit) in Berlin today, and it's steaming hot in this airless box inside a hangar; there's no air conditioning here and no fans. To wipe off their sweat, the refugees keep packs of paper tissues on one of the beds. "We use many papers because it's hot here," Kossai says.

The residents of this box are surprised to see me, a creature from another planet, but they are happy to experience something different. Me. They check me out and then, when learning from Kossai that I'm a Jordanian journalist, big smiles spread on their faces. "Sit, sit," they say. "Here, this is my bed. You can sit on it," a young man tells me.

They wish they could give me some food, they tell me, but the food in the camp is not exactly what one would give to a guest who is not a real cat.

"Why don't you sit?" a few more join in.

I ask Kossai if I can take a photo of what my eyes see.

Only if you do it fast, he says, because the guards might come any second.

Kossai, who knows this place better than I do, is afraid that the guards would eventually follow us to his box. I'll go to another box, I say to Kossai, and you stay here. I will roam the place on my own. Don't worry.

But just as I get out of his box, a couple of guards – who have been searching the place for the peeing guest – approach me. "What are you doing here?" asks the guard from Hangar 2, the one who stopped me from entering this hangar before. "I told you that you could be only in Hangar 3!" he yells at me. I make myself an idiot. What's the difference between the hangars? I ask him. Can you tell me what the difference between them is? "I don't know," he answers to this idiot, "but these are the rules!"

Yeah, rules.

Kossai joins the guard and me as I am escorted out.

Outside, near Hangar 3, Kossai says to me: "My house was not bombed by Daesh. I told you before that Daesh bombed it, but it's not true."

Who bombed it?

"Jabat an-Nusra. They bombed it because we are Christian. I can't say this here because everybody here, almost everybody, is Muslim. If I say what happened, there will be a fight here. But to you I tell the truth. I couldn't tell you this before because we were with a Muslim. Can I tell you something?"

Go ahead.

"You asked good questions, very good questions!"

What are you talking about? Can you be more specific?

"I know, my friend. My father taught me. Many things he taught me. I know." Kossai is talking about my "Jew" question at Hangar 3's guest room.

"You want to see my father? He is calling me soon."

In minutes he does. He calls from Hama, it's a video call, and Kossai shows me his papa, a man who reminds me of my father. I tell Kossai's father that he has a wonderful, smart and lovely son, but he is not surprised to hear this. Still, his eyes shine with happiness, and a warm smile spreads on his face.

I like my Syrians.

We hang around a bit more, and when it's time to leave, Kossai and I hug each other, a tight hug and a warm embrace.

Maybe one day, if our paths cross again, we will become real friends.

I exit.

Minutes later I get a message from Kossai. "It was my honor to meet you," he writes to me in Arabic.

My honor as well, Kossai.

•

Once I'm out of the camp area, I sit down. I need time to collect my thoughts, to reflect and to grasp what my eyes have just seen.

I didn't expect to see what I saw. I didn't expect a country like Germany to handle people this way.

Part of me wants to cry, and the other part wants to scream. It's sad.

What else is waiting for me, as I continue my journey?

Oh Allah, save me.

•

Where shall I go from here?

I don't know. I'll let the wind carry me anywhere it wishes, and I'll try to find my way step by step, place by place and day by day.

As so happens, I'm a big man, and the wind won't easily move me. To help the winds of Germany show me the way, I better rent a car to travel across the land.

The easiest place to rent a car in Berlin, people tell me, is at the airport. I shall do this on the day of morrow.

•

The folks at Avis rental car company at the Tegel Airport offer me a new Mercedes, one of the very few they have with automatic transmission, but I have to give them my passport. I have a digital copy of my passport, and I could email it to them, but this is not good enough for them. They want a passport, a real one, but I don't have a passport on me.

I show them a press card, but they are not impressed.

I look around, to see if I can spot a non-German who might be less "perfect," and soon I find him: a dark-skinned man. Will it be easier with him?

Let's check.

He works for a different car rental company which is, of course, fine with me.

I want to rent a car, I tell him, right now.

"I need your credit card, passport, and your driver's license."

I don't have my passport on me, but I can email it to you.

He laughs. "A picture of your passport?"

Yes. Anything wrong with that?

"Ok. Email it to me."

I leave the airport with an Opel car, an Opel Astra. I've never driven an Opel; it's time.

Where shall I drive to?

In the direction the winds take me. Let's go!

Chapter 5

Syrian Male Refugees Learn to Peel Potatoes from German Ladies

I am in Beelitz, a lovely small German town.

How did I get here? That's where the winds blew, and when I pressed the gas accelerator, Opel flew with the winds.

I get out of the Opel Astra and walk. I have feet, and at least sometimes I should use them.

It's a beautiful little place, this Beelitz, with flowers all over. Not to mention a local flower shop that I pass by at this very moment, which has flowers of every color. Gorgeous!

A couple, who seem to be pensioners, walk about with their dog. Where can I find refugees around here? I ask them. In an old hotel, which goes by the name of Pfötchenhotel and is not far from where we are, they say. Pfötchen, what kind of hotel is that? Hotel for dogs, they answer. Dogs? Yeah. It used to be a dog hotel, and now the refugees are there.

Not far from this place is a hospital where, years ago, Adolf Hitler was treated for leg wounds. How do I know? A local guy, Christian, tells me. What do you think of the refugees? I ask him. "They should go back home." To Syria? Of course, where else? Are they, the refugees, so bad? Yes, they are. "They don't integrate, they just walk here and steal things. They stole the bicycle of my friend. My girlfriend was raped."

When?

"Ten years ago."

Were there refugees living here at that time?

"I don't know."

I talk to more people here, and none likes the refugees. They say that crime has gone up since the refugees arrived, that they steal cars, and that nothing good will ever come out of having the refugees in Germany. Yes, of course, people in need should be helped but not these refugees, they say, because these refugees are nothing but a bunch of thieves.

Are they right?

Kossai didn't strike me as a car thief, nor did Tanios and his wife. But what do I know? I've just started my journey into this Refugee Nation.

"Refugees." In Britain, where I spent some time before flying to Israel, they say "migrants," not "refugees." The same people who are "refugees" in Germany are "migrants" in Great Britain. Who is in charge of coining the names? Go figure.

I get back to my car, and I keep on driving.

On a countryside road – I have no idea where I am – I see a man riding his bicycles with his dog alongside him. I stop the Opel Astra.

His name, he tells me, is Bernhard Knuth and he is the mayor of Beelitz. What does he think of the refugees, is he in favor of having them here in Germany?

"Yes."

Why?

"They are people in need, and we have to help them," he says. Hopefully, he adds, the situation in their home countries will improve and they will go back.

Do you think that peace will come there?

"I don't believe so."

So, they will stay here?

"Yes."

Do you think that Germany should keep bringing in refugees?

"Yes, I think so."

Are you talking about a limitless number of refugees, or should Germany set a limit on how many refugees it takes?

"Should have a limit."

What's the limit?

"This I can't say."

One million, two million, three million? A billion?

He laughs loudly: "Billion…?"

Are the people of Beelitz also in favor of having refugees here?

"The majority of the people here are for taking in the refugees."

I asked some people here, and they didn't think so—

"You met the wrong people."

Another person with a dog is passing by us, and the mayor's dog gets very excited. "Schnuppe, Schnuppe, come here!" the mayor yells at his dog.

Let me ask you something, I say to him, do you think that the rest of the people in the east of Germany think like the people of Beelitz and are in favor of taking in refugees?

"The majority of the people in the east are in favor of taking in refugees. There are many, many people here who are helping with the integration (of the refugees into the German society)."

The people of Beelitz and the refugees, His Honor also tells me, meet each other, communicate with each other, and do activities together. I'm not sure how they communicate with each other, given that the people here speak German and the refugees speak Arabic, or some other fancy tongue, but this is what the mayor says, and his words are stronger than any reality.

Perhaps I should mingle with some refugees now, and leave the mayor alone with Schnuppe.

I drive to the former dog hotel, and on the way I see a man walking on the roadside, carrying a plastic bag. Could be a refugee, wouldn't you say? I stop the car and start talking to him, in Arabic.

It has been some time since I last spoke Arabic, but the refugees force me to reacquaint myself with the language, for which I'm tremendously thankful. In any case, the man with the bag hears me talking in his mother's tongue, and he's happy to get to know me. He is a Palestinian, he says, and his name is Suleiman. Would he show me to his abode in Germany? Well, maybe. If I tell the guards that he and I are good friends from Munich, he says, he could finagle it that the guards would let me in.

He gets into my Opel, and he sits down, ready for the ride. Where is he exactly from? "Akka, Palestine," he says.

If you meet an Arab in Germany who tells you that he is from Akka, Palestine you can rest assured that he has never even seen that city. Akka is Akko (Acre), an Israeli city since 1948, and the Arabs who live there to this day have Israeli citizenship, and they ain't coming here.

But I say nothing. We are friends from Munich, I'm a German-Arab, and he is an Akka Palestinian. A match made in heaven.

As the car proceeds ahead, he tells me that a few days ago he caught a snake in the neighborhood of the camp and he hid it. He wants to show it to me now, and so I stop the car where he tells me to stop, but he can't find it.

Snake. Akka. Munich. Anything goes.

In good time we reach our destination, the dog hotel. We get out of the car and move toward the hotel. Suleiman talks with the guard, a bored man, and the guard lets me in. The security rule at the dog hotel is this: If you were born in Munich, you can get in. And I was born in Munich, during Bismarck's reign.

Suleiman, 39 years of age, is not doing much these days, he tells me, but he studies German, like all refugees.

This place, he says as we walk in together, is "Scheisse" (shit).

Suleiman, no doubt, is an excellent student of the German language. What else does he know in German? Well, that's about it: Scheisse. One word that says it all. And Suleiman came from Akka to study it and be able to utter it.

An achievement.

Most of the people here, about fifty altogether according to the residents, are quite young. Suleiman seems to be the oldest, at least of those I see.

There's an interesting collection of refugees in this dog hotel, in case you are curious. Here is a refugee from Majdal Shams, in the Golan Heights.

Majdal Shams was annexed by Israel ages ago, but he says it's in Syria. And, hence, he's a Syrian refugee. The German government obviously agrees.

You might ask: How does a German dog hotel compare to the Golan Heights and Akko?

Well, let's see.

The water coming out of the faucets in this Pfötchenhotel is yellowish, which is excellent for dogs. Schnuppe, I believe, would like this water. But the people here, known in this land as "refugees," aren't sure. They ask me, a Munich man, if this is the standard water that Germans drink.

What am I supposed to tell them?

I move around in the property, and I reach the toilet, a toilet that is shared by many people, and it's all wet and dirty.

Suleiman points to the toilet and says: "Scheisse!"

He got that right!

We move to the living areas, to the rooms.

The rooms have two beds each, a table, a refrigerator, and a big No Smoking sign on the doors. What are you doing in this place, beside sleeping? I ask him.

"Scheisse."

How long have you lived here?

"Three and a half months," he says, switching back to Arabic.

Hello, Refugees!

Despite the No Smoking sign, Suleiman does smoke in the room. He has to do something, after all. On his table, I see a bottle of vodka. Yes, he is Muslim, and alcohol is forbidden in Islam but "I love vodka," he shares with me, as he holds the bottle close to his heart and hugs it. "I'm tired of Germany," he says. Back there in Syria, he has a wife and two children, and maybe one day they will get out. Allah knows. Meantime, he drinks.

Suleiman has some papers with him, and he shows them to me. They are official papers, all in Arabic, and they are from both the Syrian government and from UNRWA, the UN organization in charge of Palestinian refugees.

In other words, Suleiman was born a refugee.

How so? Well, according to the UN if your grandpa or great-grandpa was born in what is now Israel and left the place before the Jews founded their state, then you are a refugee, your papa is a refugee, your children are refugees, your grandchildren are refugees, your great-grandchildren as well, and all those born of them until eternity or until the Jews die, will be refugees as well.

What does this all mean?

Here's an example: Suleiman married a Syrian woman, and according to the official Syrian papers she's the only Syrian in the family. He, Suleiman, and both their children are Palestinians, even though Suleiman was born in Syria, as were his children.

That's International Law, if you like it or not.

Suleiman, legally speaking, was born in "Akka."

Akka sounds good, Palestine sounds great, and Germany is tiring.

"Help me get out of here," Suleiman begs me.

•

Anja, walking with her baby on the streets of Schlalach, a few minutes' drive from Beelitz, says that there are too many refugees in the land. They are in a neighboring town, she says, and they are busy stealing. They go into stores, open bottles and drink from them, open potato chips packages and eat from them, and then put the packages and the bottles back on the shelves. What are the store owners doing about it? Nothing. Why not? "The police wouldn't come." Why? Because.

What does Anja think of Angela Merkel? "She (Angela) has bodyguards, and she doesn't pay the price." Will she vote for the AfD? "I can't answer this."

Why not?

It's not safe to answer this question.

Why not? Isn't Germany a democracy where people can say what they think?

"No, Germany is not a democracy, it's less democratic than the DDR (GDR, German Democratic Republic, meaning East Germany during the Cold War). If you say what you think, you won't be welcome in your own country."

•

I keep riding the winds, and I reach the town of Gräfenhainichen.

It is here, I learn, that shooting and stone throwing on a refugee house, by radical-right activists, took place earlier this year.

Blessed be the winds for bringing me here.

My Opel and I drive to this refugee house, home or camp – whatever it's called – and soon we are there.

One little problem: there's a guard outside the property, and he won't let me in.

I have to outsmart him, but how?

The surest way to get into this secure building without being stopped by security is to dig a tunnel underneath the building, the way Palestinians do in Gaza. But this method is too costly and too time-consuming, and no one will finance it. The trick I learned under pressure in Tempelhof and got better at it at the dog hotel – that of befriending a refugee – is not possible here because there are no refugees around.

What should I do?

Well, nothing much I can do unless I'm willing to exercise patience and hope that sooner or later a refugee would materialize in the area.

I wait.

Patience is a virtue; my teachers told me when I was a kid.

They were right.

In due time I spot a man in the property, walking down the stairs of an attached stairway, and I greet him. His name is Mahmud, he tells me, and he is from Iran.

My first Iranian for this journey. Until now I had Arabs, and now I have an Iranian. I don't know Farsi, but he knows English.

Great!

Would he mind, I wonder, to pretend that I am his closest friend who had come all the way from another continent to visit him?

No, he wouldn't. He has nothing better to do today and playing a little game suits him just fine.

He goes out of the building, and we enter it together.

The security guard at the entrance, an earnest German, buys our little story and I am allowed to walk in with Mahmud to visit him at his room.

Great!

On our way to his room, which is a floor or two above, I see a bunch of Syrians sitting around tables in a big room on the first floor, and two German ladies mingle among them.

What's cooking there?

I walk in.

The German ladies, I promptly find out, teach refugees the German language. Today they teach them how to say "I peel potatoes" in German. These refugees, almost all men, have come all the way to Germany in order to know how to say "I peel potatoes" in the German language. The last time these men peeled potatoes was when Suleiman lived in Akka. Where these folks come from, the women are the ones who grace the kitchen, not men, but they wouldn't tell it to the German ladies. They are bored, just like Mahmud, and any activity other than sleeping and eating is okay with them.

As I enter the room I loudly proclaim one big hello in Arabic, which is something that these refugees did not expect. They all get up to welcome the new Arab in their midst, another man who doesn't peel potatoes. We holler, we shout -- thousand and one blessings -- and the German lesson for today is over. Let the German ladies peel potatoes; the Arabs have better things to do.

To tell their story.

Everybody here has a little story to share, a complaint actually.

What's the complaint?

They don't do anything here, except the one-hour German lesson, and they want out.

This camp living is not what they expected to happen to them in Germany, and this is not what they want. How long can a man spend his time doing nothing, they ask me?

They are in this place, for months already, and they had enough. "Life is hard," they tell me.

There's one woman amongst them; the rest are young and bored males.

Now that the potato peeling class is over, they move around with their guest, ready to show him their living conditions.

As we walk, they keep asking me if I could help them.

Like Suleiman, who asked to "help me get out of here," they want this stranger to help them out of this little prison.

37

They take me to their rooms. "Here is my bed," one of them says as he points to a bed in his room. He is a cool guy, and before long he presents me with a gift: a white hat. "This is for you," he says. The hat is too small for my head, but I take it anyway.

He shows me the sum of his belongings; almost nothing, since the rest of them are far away, in the land of his birth.

He risked his life to be here.

But what is here?

These people are deeply religious people but, as one young man tells me, here you don't talk about religion unless you want to get into trouble.

Yes.

The living arrangement in this building is unusual. There are forty-one refugees here, they tell me. Afghans live on one floor, Iranians in another, and the Syrians are on top.

I'm supposed to be with Mahmud, the Iranian guy, but I left him behind and joined the Syrians. Soon enough, I guess, the guards will find out that I'm not with Mahmud, that I don't even know Mahmud. I must avoid this. And so, I tell my new Syrian friends that I have to go.

The female, a mother figure here, doesn't want me to leave before I get to see the kitchen that they all share. It's a big kitchen, and not much food is around, but empty beer bottles are all around. Are the Muslims here entirely fake, drinking the religiously forbidden alcohol? The Iranians, she says, drink beer all the time. Not the Syrians!

With the new hat on my head, I bid this real mama goodbye, just as the guard who let me in makes his way in my direction. I go outside, to continue my journey; the refugees stay inside, to peel German potatoes.

Chapter 6

Adolf Hitler: The Undead

Back in Jerusalem, in the apartment I rented in the Mahane Yehudah market, I was sitting one day with a German journalist who has been reporting from Jerusalem for the past few years. When I told him that soon I'd be traveling to Germany on a journey into the refugee world, he suggested that I meet a man whose name I've never heard.

I researched a little about this man and found out that he is one of the most reviled of people in the land of Germany. He is so reviled, in fact, that even the anti-immigrant AfD party wouldn't accept him as a member. Other people, who like him even less, told me that he is the "spiritual father" of the anti-immigrant movement, which includes AfD and Pegida ("Patriotische Europäer gegen die Islamisierung des Abendlandes," Patriotic Europeans Against the Islamisation of the West). Pegida, despised by every European liberal, is an organization that brings thousands of people to the streets of Dresden every Monday evening to demonstrate against Muslim immigration into Germany.

In short: the man is a villain.

I love villains. Yes, really. Having spent over two decades of my life in the theater world, I know that there's no good drama without villains, that no good story can ever be spun without them, and that without reviled people life, in general, would be incredibly annoying.

I must see this man.

From where I am at the moment, Opel can deliver me to his abode quite fast.

I get in touch with the man, the reviled man, and he invites me for dinner.

I love dinners!

I press the accelerator and quickly make my way to him.

•

I have arrived.

Hello, Refugees!

Let me start by telling you something about the house of the reviled man: Plain gorgeous.

Let me move on and tell you about the family of the reviled man, whom I spot next to the house: Utterly beautiful.

The name of the reviled man, if you didn't guess by now, is Götz Kubitschek.

Have you heard of Götz?

Götz is the publisher of Antaios publishing company and is also the editor of the political magazine, Sezession. In addition, he is the co-founder of IFS, Institute for State Politics, which to me sounds kind of interesting. Most importantly, Götz is a former lieutenant in the German army, and as I look at him and try to measure him up and down, he does look like an officer. All in all, let me be short here, this man is a right-wing intellectual whose attempt to join the AfD in 2015 failed, though his wife, Ellen Kositza, had just recently been accepted to the party.

Götz, admired by German right wingers, lives with his family in Schnellroda, a little town in the east of Germany.

Most likely you've never been to Schnellroda, not to mention visited Götz's home, so let me give you a little taste of the place: It looks like a fortress. Its interior, may I share with you, reminds me of Israeli bunkers near the Syrian border. Yeah.

Personally, I am not very much into bunkers, but I'm very much into food, and I'm dead curious to see what Götz will have for dinner. Is he going to have any special hate potions? Oh, that would be lovely!

In minutes, Götz shows me to the dining room.

Look at the food here, my dears!

One of the main ingredients on the table, an impressive table, is goats. Goat cheeses, goat butter, goat milk – exactly what my taste buds yearn for. Goats, in case I didn't say it yet, are my love. Yes, I love goats. In fact, I prefer a goat to a refugee. I know it's not nice to say it, but I do. To be even more honest, I prefer goats to the purest of Germans. I can't explain it, but I'm into goats. I even prefer goats to Jews, but don't tell anybody I said that. Some people are into same-sex sex, but I'm into goats. Goats, let me be clear here, produce the best of human food.

Hello, Refugees!

Try a goat product, taste it and you will understand what heaven is. Yeah. Much better than the peeled potatoes of the Syrians!

Götz's and Ellen's children, gorgeous blondes with manners reminiscent of centuries ago, enter the dining area. Each pronounces his or her name and lovingly shake my hand, and then they sit at the table.

When everybody is seated, Götz says Grace.

These children, born into the wrong century, behave with kingly manners. None opens his or her mouth unless directed to do so by the parents, and each of them is ready to serve the elders – that's me, in this case – whenever asked to do so.

Beautiful children and goat products. Is there anything better in life?

Time to taste the products, many of which are homemade.

I do.

Götz and Ellen have two goats, I understand, and beautiful Ellen does wonders with the pair. I swear. Here is a goat butter, and I spread it on the homemade bread. Oh, God! Divine!

Any wonder the Syrians and the Afghans risk their lives to be in Germany?

Once the belly got its wish and had been filled with goaty delights, I take the time to chat with Götz.

Introduce yourself, I say to the former lieutenant, hoping that he will show me some awesome tools of his trade, such as machine guns, pistols, and machetes.

But no. "My name is Götz Kubitschek," he says, "and I am forty-five years of age. I was born in Swabia, but I live here, in Saxony-Anhalt, for the past fifteen years."

The man thinks he's in the army and he gives me details of his past in of numbers and locations.

I want more than this.

Tell me some juicy stories about yourself, I ask of him. You were in the army, and you must have some stories. Something about your past that's interesting!

Hello, Refugees!

"Well, the world in which I grew up is very different than the world in which I live in the present. In Swabia, they were very conservative and richer. The schools were better, and the education was better. We studied, for example, ancient languages. In those days it was not common to go to the military, but I went, and to a very good unit, a parachute unit. I ended up in Sarajevo as a commander, leading a peace mission in Bosnia. As a result of my experiences in the army, and during my studies outside of it, I became more and more conservative. You can call me Right Wing."

Were your parents leftist?

"No. They were typical Swabian, CDU (Christian Democratic Union, Angela Merkel's party) voters. Politically in the middle. Middle of nowhere."

Going back to his youth, he tells me that he started moving rightward politically at the age of sixteen. In America, sixteen-year-olds are busy planning their Sweet Sixteen parties, but Götz was busy with other things: politics. It was then, he tells me, that he noticed how the left was wrong, and how it destroyed both the German army and the German education system.

Was there something specific, I ask him, that took place in his sixteenth year which made him think that the left was wrong?

Yes, there was. "It was in school when I and my classmates had to decide if we wanted, once we finished school, to serve in the army or do civil service. I thought that we would meet an army officer and a civil service official, hear them out and then decide which we preferred. But the school, our teachers, would not allow any army officer to talk with us, children. We could only talk to the civil service official. We were led to understand that the German military tradition was nothing but bad. It was us who started the Wars, it was us who committed genocide, and it was our grandfathers who were criminals. I knew that my grandfathers were soldiers and that one of them was a commander as well. Both my grandfathers served in World War Two; one was in the infantry, mostly in France and Yugoslavia, and the other in an air-defense unit. One of my grandfathers became a member of the Nazi Party early on, in 1933, but when his favorite uncle was sent

43

to the Dachau Concentration Camp, accused of being a Communist, he left the Party."

Now that this is out of the way, the personal yes-Nazi/no-Nazi family past that almost every German contends with upon meeting a stranger, we can come back to the here and now. And the here and now, what a surprise, is the refugee issue.

Why is it, I ask him, that Germany accepts so many refugees, more than any other European country? I assume that you don't agree with this policy, but what do you think motivates the other Germans, like Angela Merkel? Are they simply just good people?

"There is more than one reason for it; it's a mixture of more than one ingredient. The 'being good' is the first ingredient, which is one of the ways how the left sees itself. The idea is: It doesn't matter where you come from, or where you live. It's a mentality that you can live anywhere, be a German, an American or Japanese, because at the core of it we are all the same. You can be anybody you want, whatever, and all's good. This means that you can reinvent yourself, over and ever."

This is true for many people in the West, and in many countries. What I'm asking you is this: What's unique to Germany, since Germany obviously is the most open to refugees. What's unique to Germany that it behaves in this unique way?

"There are leftists all over, in many other countries and not just in Germany. That's true. But there's a difference: Germans are more serious, and German leftists take the leftist idea more seriously than other leftists in other countries."

Why are the Germans doing this?

"This is the national character of the Germans. To them, the world is not just a reality but also an 'idea.'"

Do you think that the Germans are more serious than, let's say, the Austrians or the Swedes?

Yes and no. And Götz explains it with an example. "The EU bureaucracy, a terrible entity, has ruled that for a road to be called 'county road' (Bundesstrasse) it must be at least 5.8 meters wide. The EU countries ratified it but did nothing to implement it. Not so Germany! In Germany, they immediately cut five hundred trees along the road, and increased the road's width to 5.8 meters so it would meet the EU specification." And so goes for the refugees. There's that Geneva Convention that all signatory countries must abide by, but who takes that Convention seriously? Germany. That's the law, and they abide by it.

Is he right about the 5.8-meter rule? As far as I know, there is a German law stating that the width of a county road should be 7.5 meters, but the idea is the same, and his argument does make sense.

German sense. Very German. Does that mean that Götz, who pokes fun at this behavior, is not German? Are you not German? I ask him.

Götz is no idiot, and he is not going to ignore my comment. Yes, he is German, and yes, he cares about the law, he says. But "there are other laws in this country, national laws. For example, the law which says that no person can pass the border without certain procedures applicable to all those entering the country. And then there is the law which makes it illegal for people to roam the country without having been registered first. And the truth is that foreign governments are totally shocked that Germany is not observing its own laws, and that Germans behave like a bunch of hippies who have just reached puberty."

Well, so now we are discovering that the Germans are not such law-abiding citizens, aren't we? Which is exactly the opposite of what you have said before—

It is here where Götz goes deeper, touching the root nerve of the German. "German intellectuals," he tells me, "are very proud and relieved, celebrating the fact that Germans are changing their mentality, that they are opening their hearts. Finally, they -- the Germans -- are thinking with their hearts, and Angela Merkel is called the Chancellor of the Hearts. Germany showed the world that it could open its heart, and this is celebrated by the intellectuals as a break with Germany's past mentality."

Is that why the Germans are opening the door to refugees, just so to show the world how great they are?

"That's where history comes in. Germany wants to show the world that it is not the heartless country that it is known for, but a land of a people with a great heart."

Which and what history are you referring to, World War Two?

"Exactly. Germany wants to show to the world that it learned the lesson of its past and that it has finally changed its character."

Götz is an intellectual, but quite different than most intellectuals you would find in this country. Götz is a right-wing intellectual. "German intellectuals," he tells me, "are not favorable to their own people."

Why?

"It has to do with history, German history; the guilt."

Are we talking, again, about World War Two?

"Yes."

Not that other intellectuals, in other Western countries, are satisfied with their people, he tells me, but German intellectuals are much less so.

Why?

The answer comes in two words: Adolf Hitler.

Götz explains: "He is the undead. The war against him is being fought, right now, in the most decisive manner."

In short: He is back.

"Exactly. You have to understand: the twelve years of the Reich were such an explosion of power and rage, that you needed the whole world to defeat these people, the Germans."

Coming back to earth, leaving all intellectual and ideological reasoning aside, I pose to him the most important of questions: When did you meet your wife and what made you decide to marry her?

Götz, getting shy here like most intellectuals right or left do when forced to land from their intellectual skies to the brownish earth, remembers the day they first met. He was wearing a woolen pullover made of sheep wool, and she was wearing a mini dress.

That says it all.

It's time to leave soon.
The villain and the devil I was dreaming of turned out to be a nice guy. I'm a bit disappointed, I must admit.

•

Before I leave his house, Götz suggests that I meet an AfD politician, member of the local Parliament of Saxony-Anhalt and an Islamic scholar by the name of Hans-Thomas Tillschneider. Would I like to meet him? he asks me. I say that I would. Why not?

I stay the night in a Schnellroda hotel and on the next day I go to meet the Islamic scholar in a café close by.

Hans has a goaty beard, bald head and is quite a bit taller than I am. He wears a beige jacket, orange-red pants, and stylish eyeglasses. That's the look, I guess, of a right-wing intellectual.

We sit down, order coffee, and we start talking.

I ask him if he speaks Arabic. A little, he says, and he goes on to tell me, in Arabic, that he studied at a university in Damascus for one year, from 2000 to 2001. "That was the most beautiful year of my life," he says. He would like to speak Hebrew as well, he adds, and inshallah (God willing) he will study it one day, but not now. Now he's too busy with politics, and he simply doesn't have the time.

Well, let's talk politics.

What's your opinion about the whole refugee issue in Germany? I ask him, in English.

"It's a very, very general question," Hans replies.

I like to put it very simply for my readers!

Hans rises to the occasion. "My basic approach," he says, trying to give me an answer that is indeed as simple as possible, "is that taking all these refugees is not in our German interest."

Why?

"They come from a different culture, a culture that is strange to us, and so they cause problems, cultural problems, social problems. Additionally, in most cases, they are not very qualified—"

From what I understand, at least from what I heard recently, the average Syrian makes the equivalent of $40 a month. But to get here, even just to pay the smugglers, somebody told me costs a €1,000. This means that the refugees arriving here are the richer of the society.

"Of course; they are the traders. I know many of them because, you know, before I entered the Parliament I worked in Bayreuth, and I took the train twice a week, where I met a lot of Syrian refugees and I talked to them, in Arabic, and most of them were traders."

How long ago was that?

"Last autumn. Most of them were traders who had little stores in Aleppo and in Damascus, regions that are now destroyed. They took all their wealth and made an investment in their future" by coming to Germany.

So, you are against having the refugees here because you think they are of a different culture.

"It's a tragic story, what happens in Syria but we, the Germans, are not involved in that story. When we talk about the Syrian conflict we have to talk about Hizballah, about Basher el-Assad, about Daesh (ISIS), about Russia, the United States, Saudi Arabia – but not about Germany. I ask myself, and I ask politicians: Why do we take all these refugees?"

48

Hello, Refugees!

They say it's because of International Humanitarian Law, because of human rights, and some Conventions that Germany had signed on, and because of Germany's Basic Law.

"No! We are not obliged to take all these refugees. Saudi Arabia doesn't take even one refugee. Why? Or Jordan, why doesn't Jordan take refugees?"

Why, then, do you think that Germany is taking in the refugees?

"Because our politicians are very, very stupid. And because they don't respect the interest of their own people."

He goes on to tell me that the German voters will not allow themselves to be fooled by the politicians much longer and that in coming elections they will vote for the AfD in increasing numbers, and that in each following election cycle the AfD will gain more and more votes. In practical terms, he suggests that every refugee whose request to stay has not been granted will be deported, which the German government is not doing at the moment. But as for those who came from war zones, they should be able to stay in this country for the duration of the war.

Unlike the German government which wants to integrate the refugees into the larger society, Hans says that no integration should even be attempted. There's a clash between the cultures and any attempt to integrate between them is doomed to fail. The refugees that are already here, he says, must stay in the refugee homes and camps until the end of the war. Also, Germany should work internationally, especially with Russia, in order to solve the Syrian crisis.

If the German government follows his advice, Kossai will stay in Tempelhof for the next fifty years. I, personally, really don't like this idea.

I ask Hans: Since you are familiar with the two cultures, the German and the Islamic cultures, can you define for me what is German culture and what is Islamic, or Arab, culture? What does it mean to be "German" and what does it mean to be "Arab"?

"I would like to refuse to answer this question. Why? Because I don't like to compare cultures."

Don't compare. Just tell me what German culture means to you and what Arab culture means to you. You talked about the clash of cultures and the reader wants to know what this means.

It takes Hans some time to answer this question, a question he really doesn't like, but I push him. Finally, he says: "Islamic culture is about worship, the worshipping of God. In Germany, as Hegel said, the spirit of Germany is the spirit of freedom."

What is he talking about? It doesn't really matter because soon enough he comes up with something else: "The difference between the cultures is so deep that you can't define it. There is 'Arabness, ' and there is 'Germanness.'"

What is Arabness and what is Germanness?

"They are totally different!"

Give me specifics.

It takes Hans some time to come up with an answer, but then he does: "One example is the relationship between the sexes. In German culture, as in the Western culture, we have a liberal relationship between the sexes, whereas in the Islamic and Arab culture you have separation."

This is good. Give me more examples!

He protests my insistence. "This is a question," he says, "that you have to think about for two days. This is not political stuff, this is philosophical and it's not so easy!"

Hello, Refugees!

We talk a little more, about this and that – Hans, for example, tells me that he has a Ph.D. in Qur'anic Studies – and by the end of our conversation, I go to my Opel.

Hans fed me some big bubkes during our talk and I let it pass because I wanted to see where he was going, which turned out nowhere.

What were the bubkes? He said that Saudi Arabia and Jordan have not taken in refugees, but that's simply not true. Jordan took in hundreds of thousands of Syrians, and by some estimates it took in well over a million. And as for Saudi Arabia: It's hard to know what the Saudis are doing, and not just in this case, but we can still listen to what they say. In September of 2015, the *Guardian* quoted a Saudi official as saying that Saudi Arabia "had issued residency permits to 100,000 Syrians who wished to stay in the kingdom." Maybe it's a lie, but neither Hans nor I have the tools to prove or disprove what this official says. Of course, Hans neglected to mention the millions of Syrians that were taken in by Turkey and Lebanon, for example, because this would be counter-productive to his argument.

But, honestly, I can't fault him for not coming clean with the truth. Why? Hans is not just a politician, but an intellectual as well. Intellectuals, who most often surface on the left side of politics, historically have never shown much love or sympathy for facts and realities; that's not why they exist in the world.

What surprised me, and to a great deal, was Hans' difficulty in defining the difference between the German or Western worlds and the Arab world. The liberal sexuality that he talked about is full of bull. Has he never met a German Catholic in his life, or a Texan Evangelical Christian? Has he, by the way, totally forgotten that there are also Arabs who are not Muslims?

Götz, on the other hand, defined the "German" extremely well, and I'll never forget his example of 5.8-meter roads!

Who are the Arabs, if you ask me? Oh, Allah, they are the friendliest, warmest, most imaginative people on the planet. Yeah! And, to be honest, I need a dose of "Arabness" in my system right now! Where am I going to find myself some Arabs nearby?

Hello, Refugees!

A few months ago I was in Leipzig, which is not far from here, and I passed by a refugee camp, where quite a number of refugees were strolling outside. I don't know much more about that place, but it's time I find out now.

Let's go, Astra!

Chapter 7

The Germans Treat Dogs Better Than They Treat Us

I reach Leipzig. But where the hell is the camp? I don't know. I've been to Leipzig on a number of occasions, and I like the city very much, but if you are not a Leipzig resident you can get lost in the city quite easily. There's something in the way this city is arranged that only those who failed every architecture class know how to move around in it. Who, in Hitler's name, designed this Leipzig? Don't ask me.

In any case, I remember being told that over five hundred people resided in that camp, which is a higher number than the dog hotel but quite less than the airport in Berlin.

Oh yeah, now I remember another thing, a word: Messehalle.

Yes, that's it; that's where the camp was. Actually, in the old Messehalle.

I don't like the word Messehalle and much prefer its English equivalence: Convention Center.

Now I have to find it, whatever I prefer to call it.

I ask people here and there, there and here and after a while, I find the camp.

I park Lady Astra.

Some days I call her Opel, other days I call her Astra, but she's always a lady.

I don't see anybody outside. No Syrian, no Iranian, no Afghani.

Where are the people? Has the camp emptied out of its residents while I was away?

Could be. Everything is possible in Germany. One day the Germans are into Weimar Republic, and the next day they are into the Third Reich. Go figure them out.

I walk around and smoke a cigarette. Maybe, it's always possible, an Arab or an Afghan would smell the smoke and come by to see what's on fire.

I know it sounds totally crazy, but what other choice do I have?

The cigarette is excellent. It's an Indonesian cigarette, a clove cigarette, and it's better than marijuana. Trust me on this one.

Between you and me, I don't mind to just stick around and smoke my Indonesian.

I inhale, exhale, stare at the smoke coming out of my mouth and then, beyond and behind the smoke I see a man walking.

And he's an Arab.

Praise be to Allah!

But oops, there's one little problem. This Arab, it turns out, does not reside in the camp. He is a refugee, yes, but he's not in this camp. There is another camp in the immediate area, which is much smaller than this one, but I want this big one.

Well, if I want to enter this one, he says, there's no problem either.

How so?

This Arab, a good man, volunteers to find me a resident of this very camp, help me befriend the resident and then have the resident invite me in.

These Arabs, people that I like, know how to manipulate everything, not to mention every German that comes their way. May Allah bless them.

Soon enough, thanks be to Allah, a lady walks by with her little children, and my newest Arab friend knows her to be a refugee. He introduces her to me and me to her. Her name, if I get it right, is Thawanni. She is twenty-three years of age, a mother of two boys and two girls, and she's more beautiful than anyone in the Bundestag. I swear. She is full of life, vivacious, and quick to understand the hardest of issues. Thawanni doesn't ask even one question and immediately figures out my wish: to enter the camp, and she instantly agrees to become my closest friend.

Security people are manning the camp, and they are in charge of the comings and goings in the place. Strangers are not allowed, and journalists are never to enter. But I am Thawanni's friend, perhaps even a relative, and I get in.

What a place. I have to adjust my eyes. And my soul.

Welcome, my dear, to the freakiest place on the planet!

Like Tempelhof, there are many units here, "boxes," made of lousy materials, and all are under one roof. Each box houses up to ten people, and sheets serve as doors. If you want privacy, my dear, go back to where you came from.

Wir schaffen das. We can do it.

I want to stick around in this camp longer than I've stayed in previous camps, so that I could experience life in a camp a bit better. Thawanni, a person with a million watts of warmth, is happy to introduce me to the residents of the place, and she seems to enjoy her new job as a hostess. She introduces me to many people, so many of them that I lose track of their names. Here, for example, is a couple from Iraq. "Just today," the man tells me, "a missile fell next to my brother." Where is his brother? "In Mosul, where Daesh controls everything." His wife chips in: "I love Germany. Only Germany helps us. Angela Merkel is the best. Germans are the best. They take us in; they house us, they feed us, they give us money. May Allah bless Germany. No other country is as good as Germany. Not even one Arab country took us in! Nobody took us in except for Germany. I'm thankful to Germany!"

This woman probably thinks that I am a German official and she wants to make sure that I won't send her to Mr. Erdogan.

How's life in Germany? I ask Thawanni, who doesn't suspect me of being anybody's official.

"Life in Germany, outside of this camp, is good, thanks be to Allah. But here it's not good."

What's here?

"Every day I have to take my children to the hospital."

In this camp, she tells me, diseases are man's best friend: too many of them around.

Show me the food you're eating here, I ask Thawanni.

She does.

There is a portion on the table, in an unopened plastic container. Why is it still unopened? Well, simple enough: nobody wants to eat it. She takes the plastic off to have me taste it, to see how tasteless it is. It's couscous, or something like that, and indeed it has no taste. Any of you like this food? I ask the people. "This food? This is zift, garbage, one of the men says, and everybody agrees.

Tell me, Thawanni, does your husband kiss you at night?

She laughs. How can he kiss her, not to mention make love to her, when their abode is shared by four hundred ninety-eight other people? There is no privacy here.

I ask the people how long they have been here, or in other camps in Germany.

Well, some are campers for three months, others for five, and still others for much longer.

With so many people, can you even sleep here at night?

Not easily.

I stick around longer and more, and with the passage of time the Arabs open up to me more and more. The complaints start slow, the kind I've heard before: no job, no privacy, horrible food, and nothing to do. Then Thawanni shows me the back of her neck, where her skin is of gray color. How did this happen? Viruses and bacteria in the camp, she says. Another man enters, he listens to our talk, and he shares with me some of the secrets of the place. At night, he says, there are fights here, and knives serve as tools of the fighting trade. I don't believe him; I can't believe it.

Show me, I say to him.

He lifts his shirt up, and he shows me a cut, a large cut by a knife on his torso.

It happened here, in this camp.

Oh, God.

The people living here came from lands of war, places where one group of people had nothing better to do than slaughter the other group – Iranian, Lebanese, Christians, Muslims, Sunnis, Shia, Druze, you name it – and now they must spend 24 hours a day with each other, thanks to the generosity of the German government which put them under one roof.

Imagine being one of them. Imagine that the man sleeping in the bed above you just so happened to be the brother of the man who raped your sister and murdered your father. How would you feel?

I don't know about you, but I'd feel miserable.

Time passes, and more of them open up. "The doctor told me not to eat the food here, it's food that will make you sick," a man says. "Listen to me," another man intervenes, speaking loud and his voice shakes with pain and anger: "This is a terrible place. The German government treats us worse than dogs. Dogs have a better life than us! I want out of here. I want to go back to Syria. If I could run out of here and take a plane to Syria, I'd do it today! I want out of here! Today! Today!"

Today, not tomorrow. Today, before the long night ahead; today, before the fights that will break out in the night; today, before the drugs that will be used.

The night will come soon. And in the night nobody knows how many knives will cut the flesh before the next morning arrives.

I need to go to the toilet. Where's the toilet here? I ask them.

A man volunteers to take me there.

What a sight! There is a line of toilets here, dirty and quite broken, and most of them with no doors. There is no toilet paper in any of the toilets either.

And then he shows me the faucets in the restrooms area, none of which works; there ain't no water in any of them to clean oneself.

"Look how they treat us!" he says to me, boiling with anger.

At this point I can't take it anymore. I am steaming inside of me. How can the German government allow this to happen? Have the people of this land no shame? They present themselves to the world as the most righteous of people, lovely and caring, but are they? Will they let a dog live like this? Where are we, in God's name, the Islamic State?

Hello, Refugees!

Thawanni leans on me, one hand on my back and one hand on my belly, and she smiles. I hug her tight, and I leave.

I'll never forget Thawanni, and I'll never forget this camp.

I get into my car, and I drive off.

Hello, Refugees!

Chapter 8

Did Frauke Petry Cry?

There are people in Germany who don't like Thawanni. Not that they know her personally, they don't; but still, they don't want her here. Chief among them, everybody will tell you, is the leader of the AfD, a lady who goes by the name of Frauke Petry.

I'm going to see her.

She's in Dresden, and I'm as well; it's only natural that we shall meet.

Yes, Opel Astra and the winds brought me here.

I am at Frauke's Parliamentary office at Landtag Dresden, and in minutes she appears.

In case you've just landed on earth from Mars, Frauke Petry is one of the most famous people in Germany, and one of the most despised as well. Frauke, the younger version of Marine Le Pen of France, is an ambitious lady. You recognize this trait of her the moment she enters the room, and this is quite impressive. She is well dressed, well spoken, but she's no Thawanni. You can't blame her for that; her name is not Thawanni but Frauke. No Frauke anywhere on the planet will be a Thawanni. Take it from me.

Yes, yes, I know: it's totally politically incorrect to say. But can I tell you something? Most often reality is not "correct" in any sense of the word. I bet you that when we depart, Frauke will not lean over me and put her hand on my belly. It ain't gonna happen. Not that Frauke is not a friendly lady; up close she seems quite lovely. But she is no Syrian, if you get my point.

Anyway, Frauke is the fear of many German people in high places. The main reason why the German media love to shush every time a refugee is caught doing a big crime can be summed up in two words: Frauke Petry. Not surprisingly, when she gets interviewed by journalists they usually preach to her and accuse her, instead of actually interviewing her. Some time ago I watched an interview with her on *Deutsche Welle* in English, where the interviewer did more than interviewing; he hardly let her talk and continually interrupted her. That was not an interview, but a brutal public shaming. I watched it, and I said to myself: I will never do this. Every interviewee, no matter what their opinion, deserves to be treated fairly. Sadly, many so-called journalists nowadays don't see eye to eye with me. And in Frauke's case, their bottom line is this: they don't want her to replace Mama Angela ever ever.

For the time being, they have no reason to worry. Frauke is not a "mama" in the current German imagery. She's attractive, she's quite young, and she has an excellent figure. In short: She's no Angela.

And here we are, she and I.

She is no Götz, by the way.

Better said: If Götz is the devil, Frauke is the Master Satan.

When Frauke sits down, I try to get on her good side, and I tell her that I just had an excellent Wiener Schnitzel, right here in Dresden, and that it was a really, really great Schnitzel, not like the ones they serve up north.

She laughs.

Laughter is good. And I move to business. I ask her a simple question: What does she think of the refugees' issue, is she for having them here or against?

Frauke doesn't know me personally, but she apparently thinks that I'm a German intellectual. I don't know why, but maybe it has to do with my pink glasses. These are special glasses, let me tell you. In America and Israel people who meet me for the first time think that I'm gay. In Germany, my pink glasses make people believe that I'm an intellectual. Some people, the more complex kind, think that I'm a gay intellectual.

How do I know that Frauke thinks that I'm an intellectual? Simple: I listen to her talk to me. Oh God in Heaven, how am I supposed to write what she says? I have no clue. Listen to her, the German Master Satan, talking:

"I'd like," she starts, "to go back to the year 2013. It was the AfD which then postulated in our first sort of particular agenda for the Bundestagswahl (election of the German parliament) that we wanted to separate asylum legislation from immigration legislation, because any law we have in Germany that in some ways regulates when someone is allowed to stay in Germany, for how long he is allowed to stay, and when he is not allowed to stay, is the Zuwanderungs- und Aufenthaltsgesetz (Immigration and Residence Law) which originally was thought to be also some sort of an immigration law in 2005, when Rita Süssmuth tried to introduce a catalogue of criteria for immigration into Germany, into this new law, but she failed to get majorities for her ideas. So, in fact, in Germany we have experienced over a long period of time, decades, immigration via asylum legislation. There are statistics about that. For example, many Kurds from Turkey immigrated into Germany via asylum legislation, and there are some Gutachten from people quite familiar with German legislation, saying that the German asylum legislation by itself has a problem, because it forces German courts to actually establish whether the asylum reasons in all the indicators for being or for not being asylum seeker, refugee—"

This interview is going to be torture, I can see. What the heck is she talking about? I let her talk for another minute or so, and then I cut her off. I say: I want to give it to the reader in a very simple—
      She cuts me off.
      "Yes, I know," she says, "but I'm sorry, you can cut me later on, but I have to start with the basics, because the problem in Germany is that the basics are not understood anymore. If we don't know the basics, we will not understand the complex problem. What I want to say is, if a German court has to decide whether an asylum seeker, let's say a Kurd from East Anatolia, and we have many of those asylum seekers in Germany, said the truth or did not say the truth, it's impossible to establish this in Germany. The German court system cannot possibly prove or disprove if an asylum seeker is entitled to asylum or not. And that's why we (AfD) think, that yes, we (Germans) still need to grant asylum, and we also need to care for refugees, but the judicial means that we have in Germany are the wrong ones. They were well-thought-out when they were introduced in 1949, but they are not appropriate for the current situation, that is the first thing. We mix up several terms, refugees, meaning war refugees, for example from Syria;

political asylum seekers, who could be from anywhere, but they make up less than 2% of all the asylum seekers in Germany; and then other people who are maybe entitled to subsidiary protection."

And she goes on, on and on.

We are in Germany, I know, a country whose people must discuss the legality of every little thing until his or her teeth ache from too much movement. Still, I want to channel conversation into a field that is outside of the court system and, hopefully, she'll become less brainy.

In Britain, I say to her, they say "migrants," but in Germany you call them "refugees." Why?

"That's a problem. It makes me quite angry, because it evokes emotions and also solidarity within the population. I think it's great that in Germany there is a great tendency to help people, to feel solidarity with those who need help. But many of those coming to Germany are not refugees, they are migrants, and calling them 'refugees' gives a completely wrong picture of the whole situation."

Great! She's becoming less brainy. I love it!

Let me try to clarify. From your perspective, are you okay with having the Syrians and the Iraqis here in Germany?

"Most of them are refugees, not all of them, you know."

Hello, Refugees!

Of course. But the ones who have come here from Hama, Syria, from places like that-- "Yes, of course, if people really come from war zones and have fled for their lives, I fully understand that I have to protect them. But we think that we need contingency solutions in Germany; we think that we should change our German legislation to European legislation."

This I understand, but are you okay with protecting the refugees here?

"Of course!"

Angela Merkel says the same.

"Oh no!"

What's the difference between you and her?

The AfD's position is that "it would be much better to have safe places for them near Syria." As far as she and her party are concerned, she tells me, "there is no problem in receiving some of them here, but that is not the best solution. The best solution would be to finance places nearer to home."

She's talking about safe zones, either in Syria or Iraq.

Let me ask you something. Germany has taken in more refugees than other countries, right?

"Yeah, in Europe, yeah."

Yes. Germany has taken in more refugees than any other country in Europe. The question is, why?

"This is an interesting question. Why do German politicians think that they have to allow a limitless number of people into Germany? I think it has very much to do with the question of how Germans, or many Germans, define what is morally good or what is morally bad."

She gets brainy again, this Master Satan. How do I get her out of it? I try: Why are the Germans the only ones to think like this? Is there something special in the German culture, as far as you see it?

"No, it has nothing to do with our culture. It has to do with the feeling of guilt that has been implanted into many Germans for decades after the Second World War. So when you ask Germans why Germany has to behave like this, they will tell you that this is sort of our responsibility due to our guilt for starting the Second World War."

Don't you have that guilt?

"No."

Good. Frauke is becoming simpler; she's talking about feelings. There's something unique to Germans; guilty feelings that other Europeans don't have.

As far as I know, by the way, she's on to something. About 95% of the Germans that I meet tell me that Germany is taking in more refugees than other European countries because of the "history." When I ask follow-up questions, interestingly enough, I find that "history" means different things to different people. To some it means guilt, a guilty feeling because of what this country did during World War Two. To others it's about showing the world that Germany has changed and that it is not the cruel society it once was. Then there are those who speak of their fear, a fear that other nationals would call them "Nazis" if they didn't open Germany's borders to migrants. But Frauke, as she just said, doesn't have any guilty feelings. The question is why?

You, I say to her, cured yourself of the guilty feelings. How did you get rid of the guilt? Did you go to a psychiatrist?

She laughs aloud. "First of all," she says, "I am Protestant. So, being a Protestant, you learn about Ablasshandel ("Indulgence"), you know, what Catholics used to do, paying for their sins before Luther came in, telling them that this was really a bad idea."

Becoming a bit more serious, she adds: "You see, I lived abroad for a few years, I lived in England."

Is that why you don't have guilty feelings?

"I lived three years in Britain. Many British, many Americans, and people from all over the world, those who talked with me, said: 'We don't understand why Germans have such a problem with themselves.' Also, I come from the East; I experienced a real unified Germany one time in my life. But I felt that many Germans could not even enjoy the fact of being reunited; they felt that they had to give up their national identity in favor of a European identity. But traveling in Europe, and speaking to a lot of people, I found that this was not the wish of any other

European; it is a German 'specialty.' And it all initiated my thinking."

Any history of Nazism in your family?

"Not that I know."

Uncle or something?

"My grandparents were sent to the War. My grandfather, my father's father, died somewhere in Russia. My other grandfather was, fortunately, too old to serve very long, so he was allowed to come back and stay with his family, and he was completely against Hitler."

Let me ask you another question. I met Götz Kubitscheck a couple of days ago.

"I don't know him personally. I am not really keen on him, honestly."

As far as I understand, he was not accepted as a member of the AfD.

"Yes."

Why?

"Why? Actually, we don't— I would never publicly say the reason. I am quite glad that he was not accepted."

His wife was.

"Yes, unfortunately."

How did it happen?

"Pardon?"

How did it happen that his wife was accepted and he was not?

"This is due to, sort of, the rights that political subsidiaries have. The AfD consists of 16 Landesverbände (state associations), and every Landesverband can accept members, or it can reject them."

So they could accept him as well?

"Yes, they could."

But they didn't?

"No, they did not."

What's the reason for that?

"I won't tell you the reason."

I guess it is not personal. I guess it's a philosophical reason, no?

In the face of my little persistence, she gives ground, a little bit, and tells me that for Götz the AfD is a "movement" while in fact, the AfD is a political party, and that's why he was not accepted.

This is a very lame excuse, and she knows it. And so she goes on: "I am not sure whether his (Götz's) conclusions from the Third Reich are the same as ours. I would ask him how he judges the events of 20 July, 1944 (the attempt to assassinate Adolf Hitler, led by Claus von Stauffenberg and others). That's one question that's always very interesting to ask these people, because then you find out their political view of the Third Reich."

What's your view of 20 July?

"I think it was very necessary, and it's a shame that it didn't work out. All the people who tried to fight Hitler in this way should be honored very much. My partner's grandfather took part in the events of 20 of July, but I know that some people in Germany still think—"

Do you mean your boyfriend?

"He's more than just a boyfriend, but yeah… When you want to find out how someone in Germany thinks about the Third Reich and Hitler, this is the one question – about the 20th of July – that you would want to ask him, and I'd very much like to ask Götz Kubitschek this question."

I write a mental note to myself: Contact the Kubitscheks.

Since she has brought Adolf up, I ask her something about Jews.

If I understand correctly, I say to her, the AfD voted against kosher and halal food, and against circumcision. Is this correct?

"Circumcision was not a topic. Yes, we did [vote on] the issue of kosher slaughtering, and the Party Convention decided against it. But there is still an inner-party discussion going on about it, because I think we should clearly distinguish between halal slaughtering and the Jewish version of it, because there are big differences."

What are the differences?

"The degree of professional slaughtering. From what I know, the Jews have professional slaughterers; they have professional equipment, they actually do it very quickly in order not to hurt the animals, whereas from what I learned about halal they don't do what the Jews are doing."

But the party decided on both of them?

"Yes. It did so without discussion, unfortunately. We didn't have the chance to discuss all the topics."

Did you vote against it?

"I voted against it, yeah," she says, and immediately corrects herself: "I didn't vote at all, because I was not in the room. We will reopen the discussion."

Next year?

"At the latest. There will be a lot of topics which we will have to re-discuss."

Frauke is not a "mama" like Angela is, but she is a real mama, a mother of four children. Two of them, eleven- and fourteen-year-olds, "were bullied two months ago, due to the fact that I belong to the AfD."

In what way were they bullied? Where were they bullied?

"By classmates, by people from their school who organized a group against my children, calling me a 'crazy mother' in front of other pupils. My daughter and my son didn't even dare tell me, because they tried to protect me from that sort of bullying at school."

How did you find out?

"The director of the school called me, and the teachers told me. They asked me to come for a discussion, which I did, and they spoke with my children. This really hurt me."

Did you cry?

"No, not in public."

Did you cry at night?

This she wouldn't answer. She only says that "it hurt very much."

Is this the worst thing that happened to you?

"Receiving letters from people who want to murder you is not nice either."

But this does not hurt you, does it?

"Of course it hurts."

How often do you get such letters?

"Every day."

I wonder to myself what would Frauke have said to that fourteen-year-old Lebanese girl had she asked her to let her stay in Germany.

I ask Frauke why people vote for Angela again and again (Angela Merkel is in office for over ten years by now). "Germans," she answers, "are still very attracted to authority."

As Frauke sees it, Angela is an authoritarian dressed in motherly clothes and "Germans are set to love authority, I don't think that has changed. Looking up to authority is something that is true for many Germans."

We talk for a long time, Frauke and I, and when it's time to depart she poses for the camera with me as if we were old buddies. It took her some time to warm up to me, but once she did, it was real. She is no Satan, sorry to inform you; she's German, a German lady who says out loud what the biggest German machos are afraid even to whisper.

I like this lady.

Come to think of it, so far I liked every German and every Arab that I met on this journey. Why is it, I ask myself, that without fail I like Arabs and Germans, the very people who historically have shared a bizarre tradition of hating Jews? Is this the fate of the Jew to love his enemies?

Chapter 9

Two Semites Amongst Thousands of Catholics

Talking to right-wing Germans, in between of visiting refugees is stretching my mental capacities.

I need a break.

I hear that in the city of Leipzig, the city where I met lovely Thawanni, thousands of German believers are gathering for spiritual uplifting and heavenly inspiration. Should I join them?

Hell, why not?

●

Close to forty thousand people attend the 100th German Catholic Day (Katholikentag) in Leipzig, an event lasting five days. The Katholikentag takes place once every two years and the theme of this year's gathering is: "Look, Here Is the Man."

This quote refers to the New Testament text: "Then Jesus came out wearing the crown of thorns and the purple robe. And Pilate said, 'Look, here is the man!'"

I wanted spirituality and inspiration, and I get a crown of thorns.

Maybe, just maybe, that's why many of the Germans I knew back then fell in love with Baba Buddha.

In any case, I'm here already; let me see what I can get out of it.

There are various Katholikentag events taking place around the city; I go to an event about refugees. It's a panel discussion, with six people on the panel, and the audience is made primarily of alte kakers (old folks). All members of the panel, as I've learned to expect from past panel discussions that I've attended in Germany, agree with each other. In this case, all of them are pro-refugees.

No drama. No thorns. Nothing exciting.

Outside, I meet one of the people in charge of the Katholikentag and he tells me, in an off- the-record conversation, that politicians from all political parties in Germany were invited to participate in one event or another, except for members of the AfD and the NPD (regarded by some as a neo-Nazi party). He also tells me that it's wonderful that Germany opens its doors to so many refugees because now Germany can prove how great it is, unlike the Israelis who are "occupiers" and violate human rights.

Germans are good, Jews are bad. What else is new?

Later on in the day, this man also tells me, there will be a press conference with Cardinal Reinhard Marx, who is the Archbishop of Munich and Freising, and the chairman of the German Bishops' Conference. This Marx, in short, is the highest-ranking Catholic in Germany.

A holy man like Cardinal Marx will be able to offer me some spirituality, don't you think?

At the appointed time I attend the press conference.

Five people sit at a table facing the journalists, and all sing songs of glory to these wonderful days of the Catholics.

I raise my hand to ask a question.

Reinhard Kardinal Marx

Thomas St

I start by bringing up to His Holiness' attention a story about Jesus Christ, as told in the New Testament. A woman accused of adultery was brought before Jesus, and Jesus was asked what to do with her because according to the laws of the day she was to be stoned to death. But Jesus ruled out any stoning. He said to them:

"He that is without sin among you, let him first cast a stone at her." Jesus, without whom there would be no Christianity and no Katholikentag, included in his circle everybody: be them thieves and be them righteous, be them believers and be them adulterers. To Jesus, none of us is better than the other, as all of us are sinners. How come, I ask the Holy Cardinal, that leaders of the AfD and the NPD were excluded from this event, a Christian event, in the name of Jesus when Jesus would exclude none?

"I am not responsible for this decision," His Holiness answers me. "I am not the organizer of these days (the Katholikentag). This is him," he says, pointing to Prof. Thomas Sternberg, who is sitting next to him.

Would He have included them, had it been up to Him? I ask the holy man.

"That's not a question," the Holy Man replies.

I have no clue why this is not a question, and I try to push harder, insisting that it is a question. But Holy Marx wouldn't have any of it. "It is their decision," he says, pointing to Thomas and friends, "and I have to respect them." Yep. As if they would dare to say 'no' to him, had he told them not to exclude anybody.

The Holy Man facing me has no guts to say what he thinks. He is no Frauke.

Prof. Thomas, who is the President of the Central Committee of German Catholics, says to me that "we have not excluded them." What happened, he says, is that "we have not invited them."

Were they the only ones not invited? I ask.

Theodor Bolzenius, the spokesperson of the Central Committee of German Catholics, who sits next to Prof. Thomas, cuts me off: "This is a press conference, not a debate. You had a question, we answered it. That's it."

Debate? What is he talking about?

I can't expect any of these non-holy people to offer me any spirituality. What a waste of my time.

But before I'm totally giving up on my present visit to Leipzig and the Catholics, I find myself a man who might – just might – make my return to Leipzig worth it. His name is Aiman Mazyek, and he's no Catholic. Born to a Syrian father and a German mother, kind of a German Barack Obama, Aiman is not a Chancellor but the head of the Central Council of Muslims in Germany.

Do you think, I ask Aiman, that most people in Germany want the refugees here? You live in this country, you know this country well, what is your feeling about what the people think?

"The first reaction of the people, of society, is to keep the structure of the society as it was before. If you give people the option to decide on an issue like this, they will keep the past structure in place. No one wants a change. People, for example, say: 'Fifty years ago there were no Turkish people in Germany, there was no Turkish food around, no kebab, but now every third or fourth house has a foreign name on its door.' That's human, that's normal, and this has nothing to do with racism. That's the first reaction. And then there's the second reaction. The German Christian says: you have to love your neighbor. The German atheist says: you must have solidarity with the needy. And it is at this stage that you, we, have to find the balance between these sentiments, and compromise between them. For example, a village of five hundred citizens should not be asked to take ten thousand refugees but, instead, fifty or ten refugees. We have mosques here in Germany which are suddenly packed with refugees, and people say: 'Enough!' But I say to them: What do you want, to send them back?"

Angela Merkel would not put a limit on the number of refugees allowed into Germany. Do you agree with her? Do you think that there is a number above which no refugee should be allowed in?

"It doesn't work by 'mufti' order, who will dictate: This is the limit, and that's it. Each individual makes up his own limit. There are countries, I know, that take in millions of refugees, none of which sets a limit or discusses the issue of limits. In Europe, there are six hundred million people, and it tries to set a limit of 2.5 million refugees all over Europe."

Do you think that Germany, after accepting well over a million, should say: We have done enough?

"We can't say 'Stop!' because anyone who needs humanitarian aid must be helped. But it doesn't mean that I have to house them in my town; I can put them in refugee camps as well. Many of them, by the way, would go back to their homeland once peace is achieved."

What is the reason that Germany opened its gates wider than any other European country? As a Muslim living in Germany, what do you think of it?

"Not long ago trains, busses, and cars left Germany to death camps, to Auschwitz. But now, and for the first time and for all to see, Germany is helping people who flee from death, and drives them into the country with trains, busses, and cars. And everybody in the world is watching. This is one motive, an important motive, which propels the Germans into acting the way they do. It gives them the feeling, the sense, that 'We can do it right! In the past we did it wrong, very wrong, but now we're doing the right thing.' This is what drives Merkel, and this is what drives the people of Germany."

Do you think that Germany will change as a result of having more people from the Middle East living in Germany?

"It will not change the general culture, because the number of these Muslims is not that high, but it will influence the Turkish community, in a good way, by making it more pluralistic. Where you from, Tel Aviv?"

Hello, Refugees!

How did you figure out I'm Jewish?
"I sense it; I taste it."
How did you "taste" it?
"We are Semites!"
I like this man!

Aiman is the first person in Germany to catch me, to figure out that I'm Jewish. His tongue, you see, is of the best quality in this land.
The man made my day.
Now I can leave Leipzig and go back to Dresden.

Chapter 10

What's Pegida? A Man and a Truck

Why am I in Dresden again?

The Patriotic Europeans Against the Islamisation of the West, known worldwide as Pegida, are going to have their weekly demonstration in Dresden on Monday evening. And, as usual, thousands are expected. How many thousands? It's hard to predict. Historically speaking, Pegida demonstrations number between single thousands to tens of thousands.

I have seen one such demonstration before, when twenty-five thousand Germans were marching on the streets of Dresden on a winter evening, but that was before the million of refugees entered this country. It will be interesting to see how many will come now.

Come Monday, I get ready to join the demonstration.

The head of Pegida is Lutz Bachmann, a man I never met, and I know very little about him, mostly from what I read on the Internet. For example, I read that Lutz was once a criminal and that he served time in prison as well. That's not a big deal, though. The famous New York civil rights leader Reverend Al Sharpton, also started his life on the criminal side, at least according to media reports about him in America, and today he is a holy man.

Whatever his past, Lutz is the head of Pegida, and this evening, like almost every Monday evening, he will march with the thousands. Why am I telling you all this? Well, Lutz agrees to meet with me before the demonstration.

I enter Opel, and we drive.

Once I reach Dresden's Altmarkt square, the march's starting point, I see Lutz unloading stuff from a truck at the center of the square.

The man is sweating!

I get off Lady Astra and walk toward the sweating man.

What is it that I see?

I see a truck, an old truck, with Lutz and another person by it. They take stuff out of the truck and put them down, piece by piece. Loudspeakers, posters, and several other little things that will be needed to make a stage, the Pegida stage.

I expected to see hundreds of people working together, but no. What I see are a man and a truck.

That's Pegida, if you didn't get it yet: Lutz and a truck.

Yes.

Pegida, known all over the world, is an old truck and a Lutz.

Is that so? I ask him. Not exactly, he says. Seven people make up Pegida and, in addition, there are volunteers.

Only that this is not what I see. What I see are not seven people plus volunteers, but Lutz and, oh, here's another guy, who says that his name is Sigi.

I should have a name like this. Sigi. Too late for me, I guess.

I love the sound of it: Sigi. If one day I have a goat, I'll call it Sigi. There's a famous German politician whose last name is Gysi, but it's not as good as Sigi. Sigi is much better.

What else do I see here beside Lutz and Sigi? Ahead of us, on this square, I see a line of police vans. They are here, I guess, to make sure that there'll be no trouble.

Pegida.

Hello, Refugees!

Welcome to reality: a truck called Pegida and a man named Lutz. Practically, a one-man show.

We talk.

How many will come today? I ask Lutz.

"In summer, when the demonstration takes place while there is still light outside, there are fewer demonstrators."

Why?

"Because of the counter-demonstrators, the leftists. They take photos of the demonstrators and send the photos to the demonstrators' bosses, and then the demonstrators lose their jobs."

The other way around, right wingers taking photos of left wingers, is not happening because "if you take a photo of a leftist demonstrator no harm will come his way."

So says Lutz.

"Government employees participating in a Pegida demonstration," he adds, "will definitely lose their jobs."

Will they also lose their jobs if they take part in a leftist demonstration?

"No. In fact, not only do they take part in those demonstrations, but they are also forced to attend those demonstrations."

Lutz also tells me that "last week was terrible" because counter-demonstrators "threw screws, like that" at them, and and he demonstrates with his fingers what "like that" means, about three inches. He collected, he says, between fifteen to twenty of them, for evidence purposes, and Sigi interjects and says, "I have them with me." I ask them to show me the big screws, and Lutz does.

Kind of. What he shows me are not big screws but a bunch of nuts.

If Lutz had a p.r. person working for him, he or she would never allow this to pass. But this is not what Pegida is. Pegida is a one-man show.

Lutz works while he talks, building his stage together with Sigi, but once he's done, we go to a café, sit down, and get ready to talk.

First: I order Diet Coke with ice and lemon.

That's me.

Now we can talk.

And talk we do.

We talk about German politicians with criminal records; meaning, he's not the only one to have been in prison.

And we talk about Mama.

Angela, Lutz tells me, reminds him of the "guy from eighty years ago," meaning Adolf Hitler. Angela uses her power as a Chancellor to do whatever she wants, he says, and she breaks German law. She also breaks the Dublin Regulation. According to the Dublin Regulation, Lutz says, most of the recent migrants to Germany should be sent "back to the country of first entry into the EU."

Does he want to send back the Syrians to Hama?

No.

Those who fled war zones, Lutz says, should be protected in Germany, "We (Pegida) accept all war refugees, Christian and Muslim religious refugees, or those who fled because of sexual harassment." All others, out. "We are talking about 400,000 people, who are illegally here."

Listening to Lutz talk reminds me of the average New Yorker, not to say the average Montana resident. Most Americans, Republican or Democrat, would say more or less the same about migrants in the USA. So what's the story with this Lutz that quite some people in Germany view him as a Nazi, saying that there's no difference between him and the NPD party?

What do you think of the NPD? I ask Lutz.

"I met a couple of them, and they are really simple minded."

Would you call them neo-Nazis?

"Maybe. You can call them that."

This man, judging by his words to me, does not strike me as a Nazi. But why is he dedicating his life to oppose the "Islamisation of Europe"?

Because he loves his culture, he says, and he's fed up with Germany's cultural changes. It happens all over, he argues, even in the little things of life. Traditionally, he gives me an example, every German city that respects itself has a "Christmas Market" in the weeks around Christmas, but now people are told to change the name from Christmas Market to Winter Market, to accommodate the Muslims. Why should I give up my culture, he asks?

Just recently, Lutz was convicted by a German court for incitement of racial hatred on a Facebook page that bears his name, in which refugees were referred to as animals and dreck (trash); he was fined €9,600.

Did you call the refugees "dreck"?

"The economic refugees, not the war refugees."

And for that you were taken to court?

"Yeah."

Why?

"There is no freedom of speech here."

Are you appealing?

"Of course!"

What would you like to have written on your grave?

"Just burn me and throw me in the wind. No funeral."

Shut up; you know what I mean. On the monument, over your grave: "Lutz Bachmann..." -- give me a sentence that will describe you, one that you'd look down on from heaven and smile. Imagine it: A German cemetery, right here in Dresden.

"'I'll be back!'"

The man is funny.

Hello, Refugees!

Time runs out, and Lutz has to go back to his truck, to the stage, to the Pegida stage.

By now thousands of people have arrived, all milling about the square near the stage, and Lutz must tend to them.

Sigi gives me a tag, a Pegida tag, as if I were part of the Pegida organization. I'll march with it. Why not?

We shake hands, and they depart.

I hang the tag around my neck and I light up a cigarette. The parade starts at 6:30 pm and I can enjoy another Coke.

But before any Coke has even a chance to arrive, a man on a bicycle rides fast in my direction. He approaches me, and he tells me that he wants to know who I am and he wants me to give him my business card. The man, a Nazi hunter, wants to "out" me.

Interesting, my Germans; they love to chase each other.

Music starts, then some speeches, but once the talk is over the march on the streets begins. Sunset in Dresden today is after 9 pm, which means that this march won't take place in the dark.

I join the march. Walking is good for my health, the doctor said.

The police vans follow us, driving alongside us and in front of us.

Along the route of the parade I see people with cameras, taking videos as if this march was a beautiful visual to capture.

"Merkel must go!" the marchers chant.

We keep walking, walking and walking.

Somewhere about mid-route, I go to chat with two people who record the march on their cameras on the side of the road. One, I see, has a clicker as well. What are you doing? I ask him. "I count the number of demonstrators." What for? Well, this is a project of the University of Leipzig, he tells me. Why is the university interested in this? I'm not sure.

How many so far?

"Somewhere between 2,500 and 2,900."

Less or more than last week?

"More."

The marchers keep marching until they reach the Altmarkt again, where they listen to more speeches.

Germans, let me tell you, will kill for speeches. I'll kill for a schnitzel.

I go to one of the cafés in the square and order a schnitzel and a Diet Coke, which in Germany is called Cola Light. Fatty foods, let me tell you, go extremely well with diet drinks because they make you believe that you are losing weight.

As I wait for the schnitzel, who arrives at my table? Ellen Kositza, the wife of Götz Kubitschek. She tells me that she has not been to a Pegida demonstration in a while but today, what a wonder of wonders, she decided to join the folks.

She sits down for a mug of beer, and we schmooze. I tell her about my conversation with Frauke Petry, regarding Götz's AfD membership, and that she "would ask him how he judges the events of the 20 July" (Stauffenberg's attempt to assassinate Hitler). Frauke, I tell her, believes that Götz is an anti-Stauffenberg man, and that's why he is not accepted as a member of the AfD.

Ellen is shocked. "I wonder," she says, "why she never asked my husband what he thinks of Stauffenberg. It's not a secret!"

What does Götz think of Stauffenberg?

"My husband has spoken, and in public, about Stauffenberg. He (Stauffenberg) is one of his idols. In our home, our daughter loves Stauffenberg as if he were a pop star. Her room is full of posters, postcards, and books about Stauffenberg."

Would you mind to take a photo of her room and send it to me?

"I will."

Ellen tells me that she is not accepted as a member by the AfD after all. Yes, a local AfD office approved her, but the national office denied her membership.

Oops.

This is not the only issue she and her husband have to cope with.

They have a publishing company, but it's not easy for them to sell their books. For one thing, some time ago Amazon informed them that no book by their publishing company would be welcome by Amazon anymore and it has shipped back the books that were still in stock.

Why?

No reason was given.

Yet, Amazon is not their biggest problem in life. The banks, believe it or not, are. How so? Deutsche Bank, she tells me, closed their account. Why? Because. The German Post Bank also closed their account, with no reason given. At the moment they have a bank account with a bank called Sparkasse, but this is only because they sued the bank after this one, too, had initally closed their account.

If what Ellen tells me is true, this is what it all means: If you don't think in a "proper" way in Germany, your life will be one huge sorry affair, and you'll wish to move to North Korea.

To find out if Ellen is a truth teller or not, I need a little patience. Ellen just promised me she'd send me photos of her daughter's room; let's see if she'll deliver.

Chapter 11

I Pray to Allah to Give Me a Blonde German

I take Astra, and I drive. Where to? Here and there, there and here until I see a building that seems well-secured in a place called Pirna. I stop.

Is it a refugee camp?

If some Arabs will be passing by, then it probably is.

It rains cats and dogs and no Arab shows up.

When it rains, perhaps, no Arab likes to get wet.

But Afghans do. Yes. Here are three Afghanis passing by me.

So, yes, this is a refugee camp.

I'm getting addicted to refugees, I think.

Would you be willing, I ask them, to host me at your abode?

Yes, why not.

We walk to the camp, an old building, but the guards won't let me in. The guards here are tough, and they want to protect the refugees from people like me, a white man. No visits, sorry. The Afghanis want me inside, but the guards don't. As far as the guards are concerned, the refugees are babies who don't have a mind of their own and they need to be protected from strangers. One of the guards, a tough blonde lady, stands like a statue near me and orders me to leave the camp at once.

She reminds me of blondes I saw in some horror films.

I go back to Ms. Opel, ready to drive on. But then I see a man walking by, and I greet him in Arabic. If he answers, he's an Arab; if he doesn't, he is something else, maybe a Jew.

Fortunately, he does answer.

An Arab.

Peace on you, my friend. What's your name?

"Yunis."

Where are you from?

"Lebanon."

How much did it cost you to get here?

"€2,200 to cross by balloon (inflatable boat) from Turkey to Greece."

What made you leave your country and come here?

"A Sunni shot me in the leg."

What happened next?

"For three days I was thinking what to do, and then I thought I should go to Germany, get married to a German girl—"

Why marry a German girl?

"She would teach me German."

What kind of German girl, a blonde?

"Yes."

Why? Do you think that German girls are the most beautiful girls in the world?

"Yes."

When the three days of thinking were over, what did you do?

"I sold my business, a restaurant, and decided to move out."

How much did you sell it for?

"$12,000."

He bought a plane ticket and flew from Tripoli, Lebanon to Izmir, Turkey.

How much was that?

"$1,200."

Where did you go from there?

"Ankara."

On the same day?

"Yes."

Then from Ankara to where?

"I took the balloon to Greece."

How did you know about the balloon?

"A Syrian guy told me."

How many people were with you on the balloon?

"Thirty-nine. After 4.5 hours, I arrived in Greece, where I stayed four days."

Where?

"I don't remember."

In a hotel?

"Yes."

How much was that?

"$100 a night."

And from there?

"I took a boat to Slovakia."

How much?

"$100."

And then?

"I went to Serbia."

What after Serbia?

"Slovenia."

And from there?

"I don't remember."

But how?

"Bus."

Where did the bus drop you last?

"Austria."

And from there?

"Germany."

Why didn't you stay in Austria?

Hello, Refugees!

"I got a paper that I'm from Syria, and the Syrians go to Germany."

Where did you get that paper?

"A Syrian guy gave it to me."

When you got to Germany, which papers did you give the authorities?

"My Lebanese papers."

Let me ask you again: Why didn't you stay in Austria?

"They told us that Germany was the best."

Who told you?

"Lebanese."

Did you already have the chance to visit the grave of Adolf Hitler?

"No."

What do you think about Hitler?

"I don't know history."

How many people live in the camp?

"Two hundred."

How many Lebanese?

"Only three Lebanese."

How is it in the camp?

"Nothing to do. Life in the camp is very hard. Everybody is using hashish; I don't."

Would you like to go back to Lebanon?

"Yes, but I don't have the money to go back."

And if you had the money?

"I would go back."

When?

"Today."

What is your biggest wish?

"To find a wife and have a home."

Did you see cute German girls?

"I did, but they don't like Arabs. I went to night clubs, but the German girls don't want to marry."

How do you know that German girls don't like Arabs?

"When I walk on the street, Germans call me 'Scheisse.'"

How long have you been here?

"Eight months."

Hello, Refugees!

How much is left of the $12,000?

"Nothing."

Did you tell your family how bad it is here?

"Yes. My mother and father tell me to come back. But I don't have the money."

Under his ears, he shows me, the color of his skin is different. This is from the viruses that are in the camp, he tells me.

I had heard of this before from Thawanni, who had a similar complaint.

How do you spend your time?

"I cry a lot. I go to the river, I smoke, and I cry."

Are the Germans in charge of the camp treating you well?

"Good. But life in the camp is bad. Every day there are fights. Syrians and Moroccans, Afghanis and Iranians…"

Do the police come when this is happening?

"They do."

And what do they do once they come?

"They put the people who fight in a hotel for a day, and then they return them to the camp."

Where do the people get the hashish?

"I don't know."

How much money do you get?

"€370 a month."

What do you miss the most in Lebanon?

"Everything. The country, the people."

When you pray to Allah, what do you ask Him?

"That He gives me a wife and money."

Do you have any friends here?

"Not one."

You think that Allah will help you out of this situation?

"Yes. Only He can help me."

If Allah gave you two options to choose from, a Lebanese girl and a blonde German girl, which one would you pick?

"The German blonde."

Why?

"They are more beautiful!"

Yunis touches me, deeply. I want to cry, but I don't want him to see me crying. I shake his hand, tell him that Allah will grant him health and I drive off.

Chapter 12

The Germans are Cold People

One of the things that I found interesting in eastern Germany is that most of the people that I encountered randomly spoke critically against having refugees in Germany. In Hamburg, most people reached at random were not as critical, at least not initially. Perhaps, just a theory, eastern Germans feel less guilty about World Word Two than the other Germans. Non-eastern Germans went from Nazism to democracy and were forced to deal with their Nazi past, or else no other Western country would have dealt with them. Eastern Germans, on the other hand, went from Nazism to communism and, if anything, when they joined the Western world, they were dealing with their immediate Stasi (GDR's Ministry of State Security) past, not the old Nazi past – which could explain why the eastern Germans don't have the guilty feelings that other Germans might have. Also, in the GDR's time, people were made to think that they were the good guys while the Western Germans were the Nazis; thus, no Nazi guilt for them.

Just a theory.

I'm leaving the east and am moving on to Bavaria.

Will the Bavarians be against the refugees or for them?

I'll soon see.

I reach a little town called Münchberg, and I spot a food truck that offers chicken, roasting hot inside the truck.

I've never seen anything like this before, so I park Opel and get myself a chicken.

Oh Lord: This is just perfect!!

In the middle of consuming the fresh chicken, a man passes by. He orders a hot dog, and while the hot dog is being prepared he says that not far from this truck, in the back of the red house across the street, there are some refuges. It used to be a hotel, he says, but now it's a refugee home.

The refugee-addict that I am, I go there.

Hello, Refugees!

The name of the hotel is Hotel Wauer, and it looks much better than the dog hotel.

There is a "closed" sign at the entry of the hotel's restaurant, where in the old days a menu was most likely posted, but the hotel itself is not closed at all. Behind one of the windows of this hotel, or former hotel, I see a lady with a hijab, and she's looking out.

Good sign!

Abdul, formerly of Aleppo, invites me in.

He, his wife, son, daughter-in-law and grandchildren, eight souls altogether, are sharing a room at the Hotel Wauer.

Would I like some coffee, maybe a few cookies? Abdul asks.

Of course, I do. A good coffee will go very well with the chicken in my belly, and the cookies won't hurt.

The coffee arrives.

Abdul's coffee, sorry to say, is not Tanios' coffee. It's not Arabic coffee but a German instant coffee, which I struggle to drink.

The good thing is this: the room is lovely. There are fine sofas here, comfortable armchairs, and some other furnishing. This place is not the Tempelhof of Berlin, nor is it the Messehalle of Leipzig. It's the Wauer.

We sit down, and Abdul tells me that he shares this room with another family. He also tells me that he and his family are Yazidis. Not Muslim, not Christian, but Yazidi, the kind of people that the Islamic State, Daesh, loves to behead its men and rape its women.

"Our home is Syria," Abdul tells me as if apologizing for not welcoming me in a living room like the one he had back there.

Their home was destroyed, he tells me, and so they decided to leave. They crossed the border to Turkey, walked by foot for one hour, took a bus to Istanbul, then to Izmir, and from Izmir their family crossed to Greece. It cost them, for the eight of them, $5,000 to cross by sea. They arrived in a small island, which he doesn't remember its name.

Wasn't a fun ride. He saw people dying in front of him, drowning.

Hello, Refugees!

How long did you stay in Greece?

"Six months. After that we boarded a big ship, which took us to Athens."

That trip cost him another $5,000.

"After ten days in Athens, we took a bus to Croatia, a train to Hungary, and then a train to Austria. From Austria we went to Germany."

Why Germany?

"Everybody loves Germany."

How much money are the Germans giving you?

"€320 per month for each person. We love Germany. In the Arab world, nobody cares about us, only Germany. We love Germany!"

Why is Germany giving you a home and money?

"I don't know."

What do you think?

He thinks, and then he says: "Human rights."

Do you miss Syria?

"They slaughter us there. Could I miss it? Every day they slaughter us, every day. In ar-Raqqa (city in Syria, which became the "Capital" of the Islamic State in 2014), they brought girls and women to the market and sold them as sex slaves. That's what's happening in Syria today. That's why we left."

Did you see it?

"On TV."

What do you think of Assad?

"Very good. He was very good to us."

Do you have German friends?

"No. We are here by ourselves."

We talk a bit more and then go outside to the yard, where residents of this hotel, all refugees, sit to smoke and to stare at the sky.

And I see Ahmad.

Ahmad is a young father from Syria, and he seems to be the kind of a guy who knows no fear and will say whatever is on his mind.

I talk with him.

He was a car electrician back home, he tells me, but here he's doing nothing. He's not allowed to work, he says, because he doesn't know German, and he doesn't know German because there are no German courses to study. In short: he's potzing all day. He lives with his wife and child on the second floor, and his wife stays in the room all day. "She wouldn't come down here," he tells me.

Why?

Because.

What's your dream?

"To go back to Syria."

When would you like to go back, today?

"Not just today; now. Now, at this minute. Let the winds take me, my wife and my child to Syria now, right now!"

Why don't you fly there?

"When the war is over I will."

Ask your wife to come down, Ahmad.

"She won't."

Don't give up; try.

He calls her, she shows up at the window of the second floor, but she wouldn't come down.

"You see; she wouldn't come down."

Ask her again.

He does, but she stays up there.

Try again. Ask her until she does.

He calls her again, and again, and finally, she comes down.

She is a beautiful lady, dressed with a hijab and her divine smile lights up the whole of Münchberg.

Abdul asks me if he could invite me to lunch.

My belly is full, but I can't say no to this man.

Excellent food, let me tell you. Especially the tahini. I never, ever ever, ate such an excellent tahini.

This tahini is mixed with honey, and it's just perfect. In former times, I'm sure, kings were served this tahini.

In the middle of the meal, a blonde woman walks by, totally surprised to see me.

Who is she? I ask.

94

Hello, Refugees!

She's Mrs. Wauer, I'm told, and she owns this hotel.

Abdul and family invite her to join us, but she says that she ate already. Still, she sits down to offer us more company. She likes the Syrians, she tells me, more than the other refugees, and she will vote for Angela Merkel in the next election. It's very good, she says, that Germany keeps an open door for the refugees.

Why is it that Germany is welcoming more refugees than any other European country? I ask her. In reply, this lady doesn't mince many words. "Because of Adolf," she says.

Abdul, who doesn't understand a word she says, as he doesn't know any German, proclaims for all to hear: "The Germans are good, they help us, they love us."

He repeats this line again and again and again. It's heartbreaking to watch.

•

I go back to Astra and drive to the picturesque town of Gößweinstein. It is a gorgeous town, and it's a pleasure just to drive through it, but when I reach a hotel called Fränkischer Hahn I stop. Is this like the Wauer hotel? I ask myself. I get out of Miss Astra and proceed to the hotel, where I meet Herr Haselmeier, the owner. There are thirteen refugees in his hotel, he tells me. Five are from Ukraine, and the others are from Eritrea, Ethiopia, and Nigeria – all paid by the German government.

Brigitte, his wife, comes in with a pot of coffee.

Why is Germany opening its doors to refugees more than the other countries? I ask her.

"Because this is the German law, the German Constitution, to help people in need."

Why does Germany have such a law and the other European countries don't? I ask her. I don't know if this is indeed the case, but I say it anyway.

The German Constitution is a result of "World War Two and Germany's history with the Jewish people," she answers. "Germany will never close its borders to people who need help."

I paraphrase her answer: So, because the Germans killed Jews in the past, they are opening their borders now. Correct?

She doesn't like the way it sounds. "No. You speak for AfD or Pegida," she says.

I don't know what she means by that, but I don't push back.

I drive a bit more and stop next to a café, where I meet Esma. Esma is Turkish, Muslim, and when I ask her if she's okay with having refugees come to this land she says that she is okay with it, at least when it comes to Syrians, but not Afghanis. What's wrong with the Afghanis? Her husband is a cop, she tells me, and he told her all kinds of stories, bad stories, about the Afghanis. For example: If their request for a residence in the country is denied, he told her, they walk around and steal.

Esma wears a t-shirt that does not cover her arms, and she wears no hijab. Do you believe in God and Mohammad? I ask her.

"Yes, of course!"

Why don't you wear the hijab?

"When I get older I will, I think. My mother started wearing the hijab when she was forty- years-old."

Which woman is more sexually attractive, the one with a hijab or the one without a hijab?

"With!"

Why, then, don't you wear a hijab?

"I already have my man!"

Is your man a blonde German?

"No! He's Turkish."

Did you ever date a blonde German man?

"Yes, I did. For six months."

And…?

"It didn't work out."

Why?

"Germans are cold people."

I have pity on the Germans. They try so hard to be beloved, but even those who live with them don't like them.

Chapter 13

Are You Suicidal? The Psychiatrist Will Be Happy to See You in Twelve Months

Nuremberg: a city at the center of Germany, a city with an unforgettable history.

I am in Nuremberg. Opel brought me here.

Nuremberg is most known to outsiders for the racial Nuremberg Laws, enacted during the Third Reich. It was here where Jews, and others, lost their right to be called German and their citizenship revoked.

Times have changed. Nuremberg today is very different, of course, and Nuremberg wants to be known as a great city, open to all.

It is here, in this very city, that I meet Ramin and Hakim (not their real names), two young Afghani refugees. Both asked for political asylum; Hakim got it, but Ramin's request was denied.

I meet the two Afghanis at the Bavarian Refugee Council, an office staffed by German activists, mostly quite young, who are very dedicated to protecting foreigners from evil people, otherwise known as "Germans," and especially German government employees who wouldn't grant asylum to all foreigners.

How is life in Germany, Hakim?

"Super."

What's so great in Germany?

"Everything. In Afghanistan, every day there are bombs."

Why are there bombs?

"Because of the Taliban."

Ramin says: "Because of the Americans."

At this point, so early in the game, Hakim says that he must leave. Why? He is going for a walk with his girlfriend.

Where will you go with her?

"In the city."

What will you be doing while walking?

"Buy things for her."

What?

"Clothes."

What kind of clothes?

"Everything."

For example?

"Shoes, shirt, gown."

How long have you been dating?

"Three, four months. I had a fiancée in Afghanistan, but she can't come here, so I marry someone else."

The trip from there to here, he tells me, cost him €14,000.

How did you get that money?

"My father sold an apartment."

Why did you come to Germany?

"I have a blood disease, which in Afghanistan there's no medication for it but here, in Germany, I get it. I have to get an injection three times a week, and each injection costs $1,000. Here the government is paying for it."

In other words: this guy applied for injection asylum, and he got it.

Taliban shmaliban, all tales.

•

Alexander Thal is the representative and spokesperson of the Refugee Council, an NGO with a yearly operating budget of half a million euros. Who is putting up the money? The Council, Alexander tells me, gets its money from 750 people who donate between 30 to 1,000 euros a year because "they think we're doing a good job."

Most of the Council's work involves communication with politicians, lobbying, and press work, but directly helping the refugees is also part of its mission. Ramin, for example, showed up at the Council with an official letter from the welfare office of Bamberg, notifying him that his monthly welfare of €328 will be reduced by €41.16.

Reason?

Hello, Refugees!

Alexander reads for me from the official letter: "It is possible to get used, free clothes in different locations in Bamberg, and therefore we reduce your social welfare money by €20.41. In addition, Bamberg is a small city, where you can reach every place by foot or bike, and therefore you do not need a ticket for public transportation. Reduction: €12.74. €8.01, for miscellaneous food (snacks, etc), is also reduced."

Alexander wants to show me how bad the German government is, but I don't understand something. If Ramin must leave the country, how come he's getting paid at all?

It's complicated, Alexander answers. Ramin's application for asylum has been denied, he says, but the German government cannot deport him because he has no passport.

What did you do with your passport, Ramin?

"I never had one. I went from a country to a country with the help of smugglers."

And so, now he is in limbo: not a resident and not a non-resident.

Alexander tells me that people like him get a paper called Duldung (toleration), which they must renew every six months, and during that time they get housing and social welfare money, plus health care, for free. According to Alexander, there are 300,000 people in Germany with the same status, and one-third of them are in Germany for over six years.

Ramin, 25 years of age, lives in a refugee camp for four years by now. There are three hundred people living there.

Ramin, is this life?

"No."

Why, then, do you stay in this country?

"I can't go back to my hometown in Afghanistan because the Taliban will kill me."

Why don't you go to Kabul, which the Taliban do not control?

"They do. The President of Afghanistan, Ashraf Ghani, is a Talib (singular form of Taliban)!"

Why did you come to Germany?

"I was in Sweden. I had a false ID. But Sweden is too cold."

Why not Italy?

"They don't have the money to help me."

Do you like the Germans? Do you like their culture?

"Yes."

What's German culture?

"Beer festivals."

Aren't you Muslim?

"Yes, I am."

As a Muslim you are not allowed to drink alcohol, so what's the point?

He doesn't supply an answer.

Do you have a question for me?

"Yes."

Ask.

"Who is paying Daesh (ISIS)?"

I don't know.

"I do."

Who?

"The Jews, America, and Saudi Arabia are sponsoring Daesh. Daesh soldiers are trained in Israel."

How do you know?

"I have the information."

Who gave you this information?

"My friends lived in Syria, and they gave me the information. I also know, by a Syrian guy who told me, that a video was found in the White House showing that Americans and Israelis are training Daesh."

Do your Afghani friends think the same?

"Yes."

These Afghans don't get even close to the average Syrian that I met so far. They are hateful with no sense of humor, and their lies lack the flowery imagination prevalent in the Middle East. If they are a true reflection of their ethnic group, there's no wonder why Esma and Mrs. Wauer prefer the Syrian refugees.

Hello, Refugees!

The people who make up the Refugee Council, who have been listening in to my exchange with the two Afghanis, didn't bother to stop Ramin from airing his anti-Semitic rant about Israel and ISIS. They view themselves as absolutely anti-racist, but their deeds today didn't support it.

What drives them?

To understand them better, I ask Alexander why he is dedicating his time to do what he does. "Good question," he answers.

And what's the answer?

"Long time ago I believed that the German authorities did a good job and that the refugees in this country were given everything they wanted. But after my first visit to a refugee camp, in 1998, I was shocked."

If the Germans are so bad, why did they allow so many refugees to come in?

This question is a tough one for Alexander, and he asks for some time to think about it. He promises that he will contact me in a couple of days to deliver his reply. Will you shake hands on this? I ask him.

He does.

This exchange reminds me to check if Ellen Kositza sent me the photos, as she promised that she would do.

I check.

Hello, Refugees!

Well, she did early this morning. She sent the photos of her daughter's room, and Stauffenberg is featured there lovingly.

The lady was telling the truth.

I was surprised to hear what Alexander told me about the bad state of camps in Germany in 1998. If he's right, I'm shocked too, because this means that what I've seen in refugee camps in this country is an old practice.

•

Back in Berlin, the national Parliament of the Republic of Germany, the Bundestag, declared nearly unanimously that the 1915 killing of Armenians by Ottoman Turks was a "genocide." This is the first time that the Germans feel comfortable enough to accuse Turkey of having committed genocide, and I wonder why now?

Maybe, just maybe, the refugee-embracing Germans feel so good about themselves that they are comfortable enough to accuse another country of crimes against humanity.

•

If you drive the roads of Germany and stop next to ugly buildings, there is a big chance that you have just reached another refugee camp.

Here's a building you would rather not live in, at Kunigundenstraße 75 in Nuremberg. It has no guards in front and no tough blondes inside, but a young woman who is walking towards the entrance. Her name is Samah, she is twenty-eighth years of age, she hails from Syria, and she is happy to see me.

The refugees living in this place come in multiple colors, white, black and brown, and there are 170 of them. Some are Arabs, some are Ukrainians, and there are Africans as well.

Samah leads me up the stairs to her room, which is on the third floor, and she is crying. Daesh took her home, she says, and her parents fled to Iraq.

She chose to flee somewhere else: Germany.

Hello, Refugees!

Samah made much of the way from there to here by foot. In one country, Bulgaria, she was arrested and put in jail for one month. There, she says, she was beaten and sexually abused.

Back home, in Syria, where she witnessed death and destruction, she hoped life in Germany would be great, maybe even paradise.

It's not.

Life in this building, she tells me, is horrible. She points to the toilet, which serves twelve people, and where viruses, she believes, find rest and multiply. When we get to her room she exposes her buttocks to show me a skin disease developing there, some change in color. She thinks this disease originated from a virus in the toilet.

What's the story with skin color changes that I encounter over and over in refugee camps?

I don't know.

Samah is Muslim, and showing me her exposed behind is not something she is used to do in front of a man passing by. This lady must be suffering so much that she forgoes her traditions.

She has had multiple operations, she tells me, and going up the stairs is very painful for her. She asked to be moved to the ground floor, but nothing happened. I'm thankful to Germany, she says, and all I ask is that they put me on the ground floor and give me a private toilet.

She cries.

It's heartbreaking.

Like many other refugees, Samah walks around with official papers, medical papers in her case, and she would like me to read them. In one of the papers, signed by a German doctor, I read that she suffered a mental breakdown and that suicidal tendencies cannot be excluded.

The doctor signed on this document, dated four months ago, writes that from medical perspective, staying in a refugee camp will worsen Sama's condition.

"Please help me," she begs.

We go downstairs, passing the men's room. Oh heavens, what a stench!

Hello, Refugees!

On the ground floor I meet the refugees' social worker, a German lady, who knows everything there is to know about Samah, and she tells me that Samah needs to be treated by a psychiatrist, but that the waiting time for a psychiatrist is one year. Why that long? "There are over one million refugees, and there's nothing we can do. We are doing our best."

If I understand this correctly, next time Samah entertains a suicidal thought the doctor will see her in one year's time.

What's going on with the Germans? Can't they get anything right?

Germany has made a glorious name for itself by opening its borders to these refugees, but by not planning ahead what to do with the refugees once they were here, it sealed their fate. What the refugees go through in the camps – be it the never-ending boredom or the horrifying knife fights, the broken toilets or the tasteless food, the misplacement of yesterday's enemies in one room or the lack of hygiene in any room, will affect the refugees for as long as they live. Samah, and hundreds of thousands of her countrymen and -women, are doomed to mental and spiritual death. Yes, Germany might have saved their bodies, but it is killing their souls.

Once I'm out of the building a thought comes to my mind: Let me track the refugees right as they enter Germany. I don't know if the German border crossings with Austria, for example, are open or not at this time but if they are open and refugees are crossing into Germany through them, I'd like to ask the refugees what they expect Germany to be. When their predecessors arrived in Germany months and months ago, the images on various TV stations showed young Germans greeting them with teddy bears. Do the new refugees expect teddy bears?

I go back to my car and drive on. On, on, on, and on.

Chapter 14

Be Careful! A Refugee is Popping Out of Your Toilet!

Passau, Pocking and Schärding, a truck driver tells me, are three cities on the border between Germany and Austria.

Like an eagle on a testosterone injection, I reach Passau in no time.

Oh, Passau: What a beautiful place! Passau is a picturesque city that does not stop satisfying the eye in its immense beauty. I drive its narrow streets, each more gratifying than the other, and stare at the gorgeous houses and the awe-inspiring landscapes that reveal themselves each passing moment. And at this special hour, may I add, each of Passau's daughters walking by is more beautiful and ever sexier than the other.

Hey Yunis of Lebanon, pray to Allah to put you on the wings of an eagle and fly you here!
There are no females, ya Yunis, more beautiful than the ladies of Passau!

Oh, Passau, who created thee?

After taking in all that beauty, I reach the crossing point between Austria and Germany. Not one soldier, not one policeman or woman, nor one refugee do I see.

Same goes for Pocking and Schärding.

Stupid me! Why didn't I think of it? The gates to Germany are locked far away from here. Smart Germans, smart Angela. The whole world can witness Germany's wide-open gates, but none sees the closed gates far away, be them in Turkey, Hungary or wherever.

•

Hello, Refugees!

The job of making Germans appear better than other humans is never done, for there is always somebody out there ready to outsmart all others.

These very days floods inflict many German cities, and the issue of flooding takes up much of the public attention.

A good time to stage a little show, wouldn't you say?

An Austrian TV station wanted to film a cleanup operation in the city of Schwäbisch Gmünd, in which they were told that refugees were participating. But they had arrived too late.

Was their trip for naught? No.

Helped by local officials, they decided to stage a fake flood cleanup operation with refugees and film it, for the purpose of showing the refugees helping out and, consequently, to show everybody out there how Germans and refugees are eternally embraced by love, hard work, dedication and mutual admiration.

Ja.

•

Christian Springer, so I hear, is a great Bavarian stand-up comic and on this very evening, he will be presenting a comedy show about refugees in Neustadt an der Donau.

Should I go?

Why not!

Ready Astra?

Ja, says Opel.

I usually don't take the highways. I want to stop in little towns and chat with people, which I can't do while on the highway. But given the fact that the show starts in about an hour or so, I take the highway; otherwise, I won't make it.

Have you ever driven on German highways? If not, you should. Especially if you want to experience driving, let's ay, 120 m.p.h. Get yourself a car, if you don't already have one, and drive. It's an experience! In the USA, and most everywhere else, you would get your license revoked or have to serve five years in a dark prison cell for such an act, but not here. The land that welcomes refugees also welcomes fast drivers.

Hello, Refugees!

I'm sure you won't be surprised to know that I arrive at my destination faster than the American President could have arrived with his Air Force One.

The problem with Muslims, Christian says to the audience, is that they don't know how to swim. If they knew, they would have swum their way from one ocean to another and come out into Germans' homes via the toilet pipes. Yes, you will open your toilet lid, and right there in front of your eyes a bunch of refugees will stare up at you.

Funny.

The funniest moment in the show so far.

But then he gets serious.

The refugees coming to Germany, he tells his audience, is not a problem. If there's any problem anywhere, it is with the Germans who don't like the refugees. What are the Germans afraid of? he wants to know. Some Germans are afraid that their culture would be destroyed by the refugees, but they are dead wrong. Why? Because there's no "German" culture to speak of. The only thing that's uniquely culturally Germanic, he argues, is going for a walk after a meal.

What else is the culture of the German, beer? Beer was invented by the Babylonians, and the first beer tent had a crescent over it. In fact, if I get him right, everything in Germany originated in Babylon, Syria, Turkey, and God knows where else.

He should have met Ramin of Nuremberg, who explained German culture as "beer festivals." Had Ramin been here, he would have have moved to Turkey immediately.

The Middle Eastern refugees, on the other hand, have a culture, Mr. Christian declares.

With a name like his, I don't doubt that he understands Islam better than anybody.

Christian goes on to teach his listeners a chapter in history. No, he says, don't say that Muslims pose a danger to Germans because of all those martyrs who blow themselves up all over the world in the name of Allah. The first-ever reported suicide killing, he argues

108

with passion, was not in any Islamic literature but the Bible, in the Old Testament, and the name of the first suicide killer is not Mohammad but Samson.

Nice try, but this Christian doesn't know the Bible either.

The fact of the matter is that the Biblical story of Samson, a magnificent tale of love and betrayal, lordship and enslavement, has nothing to do with martyrdom. But this is a detail that Rev. Christian neglects to mention.

The stand-up show, which is billed as a Cabaret Solo, lasts for almost three hours, including intermission, and is as far from stand-up and cabaret as the heaven is from the earth. It is a sermon. Here is a man who stands on the stage and preaches to his audience, telling them they must embrace the refugees or else.

The audience, a couple of hundreds of people, are not complaining and none is leaving -- at least as far as I can tell. Anywhere else in the Western world you can bet your bottom euro that at least half the people in the audience would be leaving after ten minutes, but these people don't.

Why do they stay?

Perhaps that's German culture, a thought comes to my mind as I leave.

It is interesting to see and hear, over and over, again and again, white people who pretend to be in the know and will defend Islam and Muslims at all cost. The naked truth is that much terror is done in our day and time by Muslims in the name of Islam, but the Islam apologists and protectors – many of whom are sworn atheists – won't admit that at present time too many Muslims have gone nuts, in almost every Islamic country and in non-Muslim countries as well.

Why is this happening now?

For centuries, Christians have been murdering people in the name of Love and Mercy, but most of us tend to forget it. Fast forward to our time, when Christians are busy enjoying spaghetti in Rome and Buletten in Berlin, Muslims are even more busy slaughtering people all over in the name of the Merciful God. What's going on with them, the Christians and the Muslims, and why are they changing roles? Well, human societies go through phases, and followers of religion – of whatever kind and sort – are no exceptions. We are all destined to go through such cycles, believer and atheist alike. That's life. We, humans, are not as perfect as we would love to be.

Chapter 15

If You Quote Me by Name, I'll Sue You

I take Lady Astra and drive. Direction: Where the winds blow.

Where do the winds blow?

The town of Fahrenzhausen, where I meet Eike.

And Eike likes to download what's in his heart to yours truly.

There are many old people in the country, Eike says, Germans who have given their best years to the society, and the society should take care of them. But Germany can't take care of its older people because the money in Germany's coffers goes to the refugees. Germany has accepted over a million, and that's more than enough. Now may the other nations do their part, he says.

Why did the Germans accept more refugees than the others? I ask him.

"History," he says. If the Germans did not allow all those refugees in, he explains, everybody everywhere would say that the Germans are Nazis.

I've heard the "history" argument, in one variation or another, many times and today it 'hits' me. Germans accept refugees more than any other European country because they want the people of the world to love them. What do the refugees want? When I visit the refugees, what I hear most often from them is this: "Help me."

The refugee story in Germany, as it unfolds in front of me, can be summed up in four words: "Love me! Help me!" Two people, the German and the Arab, beg us to love them and to help them.

Isn't it a sad story?

•

The story gets sadder once I reach Munich, Bavaria's capital.

Hello, Refugees!

Late at night I sit down at a local eatery and talk to a young guy, who tells me that he is acquainted with a couple of security men who work in a refugee camp near Augsburg.

"They told me what's going on there," he says.

What?

"Women (refugee women) offer sex to the guards for twenty euros, or for ten."

For what purpose?

"To earn money. What else?"

And he tells me more.

"They also told me about refugees attack them. I don't know why."

Did they tell you if these things happen frequently?

"They happen often."

•

On the next day it's sunny and warm, a pleasant day to go for a walk in the university area and chat with some fresh meat.

It is a beautiful area, with many sidewalk cafés, and I sit at one such café next to two attractive female students, one with a dark hair and the other with a blond hair, and we talk about this and that. The students tell me that Angela Merkel is right: no limits should be set on the number of refugees allowed to enter this country.

I ask: One million, two million, three million, four million, five, six, seven, eight, nine, ten -- anything goes?

Not ten million, says one of them, and the other agrees.

In general, I notice as I keep talking with them, whatever the one with the dark hair says the one with the blond hair agrees.

I ask the dark-haired: If ten million is too much, how about eight million or nine?

Whatever the number, she now tells me, you can't say "no" to a refugee. Twenty million,
fifty million; who counts? If you set a limit of five million and then another refugee shows up, what will you do, let him die? Of course not; you let him in.

Hello, Refugees!

Why is Germany taking in more refugees than the other European countries? I ask her.

Because Germany can afford it, unlike other countries, comes the reply.

Can't Great Britain afford more refugees? I heard that they are rich people.

There's a "reason" why Germany takes in more than the others, she says.

What's the reason?

If Germany wouldn't do that, says the dark-haired one, who is a law student, people abroad would say that Germany is a Nazi state.

She is a tough lady, this law student. If I quote her by name, this future lawyer tells me, she will sue me.

It is at this point that I ask myself: Who needs whom more: the refugees the Germans, or the Germans the refugees?

On a nearby street, I see two handsome male students, Constantine and Robert, and I ask them if they would mind sharing with me their thoughts about refugees and Germans.

They gladly agree.

At least these guys are not going to sue me.

Neither of them is a future lawyer. Thank God!

They talk. They love to talk. Both of them tell me that they support allowing all the refugees into Germany, but they don't agree on where the limit should finally be set, be it two million, ten or whatever.

Why is Germany taking more refugees than other European countries? I ask them.

"History," they both answer. If the Germans didn't accept all the refugees, they would be called "Nazis" by non-Germans, and that's why Germany's gates are wide open to the refugees.

These pals talk exactly like the gals, but they have something else to add. As they see it, both of them tell me, Germany behaves better than any other country on the issue of refugees and human rights.

Hello, Refugees!

Your statements are contradictory; I tell them: if Germany's refugee policy is a result of a fear of being called "Nazis," then Germany is not "better" than any other but just more fearful than all others. Isn't it so?

Instead of a reply, Robert, a tech management student, tells me that he thinks that I'm of "Jewish origin." How so? Because I'm critical of him and his country.

Say what?

Well, I shouldn't be surprised. This is Germany, and having the "Jew" word thrown into the air for no obvious reason is not out of the ordinary, to say the least.

Constantine, a political science student, also tells me that Israel is an "aggressive" and "inhumane" state.

Robert agrees.

How did they arrive at this conclusion? Two years ago or so, Constantine tells me, a Palestinian killed an Israeli and Israel responded with a military action that killed about thirty-six Palestinians. Neither of these pals, by the way, know more details about that story.

In short: The Israelis, meaning the Jews, are inhumane and the Germans are angels.

I leave them, the two Jew haters. Perhaps, I think, they should study law.

I wanted to hear what the Bavarians will say, and I got my wish. For my money, I prefer the Eastern Germans; they, at least, did not pretend to be holier than Mohammad.

•

Yesterday, latest today, I was supposed to get a response from the refugee consultant and Afghan protector, Alexander Thal, as to why Germany has taken in so many refugees. But, unlike Ellen Kositza, he doesn't keep his word.

•

I get into the belly of Astra and drive to the Bayernkaserne, a refugee camp, in Munich. Let me see how the angelic Germans of Munich treat their refugees.

Across the street from the camp I meet Omar, an older man making his way to the camp. Life in Syria was good, he tells me, but in the camp, it's not.

What's the problem?

There is not even a TV or internet in his room, he says.

He lives in the camp for seven months and hopes the war will end, so that he will be able go back.

Omar is the only one of his family in Germany. Everybody else is back there in Syria, including his two wives.

The food in the camp is bad, he says, but he doesn't blame anybody for it because the cooks are Germans and Germans don't know how to prepare good Syrian food, which is the greatest food in the world.

Overall, he shares with me, the trip from Syria to Germany cost him $1,500.

A bargain!

I would like to see his room, I say to him, and he immediately agrees to show it to me.

We advance toward the camp, but the guards won't let me in. Why? Visitors are not allowed at this camp. Period.

Are they hiding anything?

•

Later in the evening I meet Anja, a twenty-five-year-old social worker who is into tattoos and piercing. She works in an institution for the prevention of sexual abuse of children, and as part of her job she worked at the Bayernkaserne last year. One of the cases she worked on was that of a seventeen-year-old refugee who sexually abused his roommate, of the same age, at night.

What did he do to him?

"He raped him. I don't know the details because when he said it to us, we tried to stabilize it and not go deep into it."

How did you stabilize it?

"I asked the guards to move one of the boys to another container, but they couldn't do it. Instead, they moved him to another room."

What's a container?

"It's like a house, a block, with ten or twelve rooms in each."

How many people in a room?

"Twelve."

Did you deal with more sexual cases there?

"Not me personally, but others did."

How's life in the Bayernkaserne? Is there any privacy?

"No. No one would let German children in such camps."

Why do you think Germany opened its doors to refugees more than other countries?

"I want to believe it's because we are good people."

•

What is more German than Bayreuth, the city of Wagner and Wagner music?

Yes, I am in Bayreuth.

Three men, all good Germans, sit in the center of town and drink beer. I join them. Will be interesting to see what comes out of their mouths now that beer has quenched their thirst.

Let me talk to them about refugees. What else?

Hello, Refugees!

Helmut, a physicist, says that he's for refugees. A million, two, maybe even three or four million. Whatever. Let them in. And then he adds: "I'm not the typical person."

What do the typical Bayreuth people think?

"Fifty, fifty," he says.

Hans, his beer buddy, is part of the other fifty. "Let them (the refugees) go to where they came from," he says.

There's another friend here, also a Hans, and he says: "No comment." But then, he adds, sarcastically: "Let the Germans out, and let the refugees in."

He and the first Hans think alike.

Like so many others, Helmut says that Germany's generous welcome of refugees is grounded in "history." The Germans feel guilty about what their countrymen and women did during World World Two, and that's why they do what they do about the refugees. But, he adds, the War period affected not only the Germans but also the Jews.

How did it affect the Jews?

"They are hard."

Could you give me an example?

"Gaza is in ruins."

Who caused Gaza to be in ruin?

"The Jews."

Why did they do it?

"The Palestinians threw rockets at them and the Jews fired rockets back at the Palestinians."

And this makes them "hard"?

"Yes."

What should the Jews have done? Should they have 'accepted' rockets and not shoot back?

"Yes."

Why so?

"What did Jesus say? Jesus said: 'If someone slaps you on one cheek, offer the other cheek also.'"

I should slap him on the face, just to see what he'll do, but I have pity on him.

Hello, Refugees!

Yes, Anja dear, the Germans are good people. The question is: Why is it that the good people who care about refugees, and about human rights in general, somehow are unable to view Jews as human?

•

I sip a little Cola Light while searching on my iPhone to see what's new in the world. Here it is from the BBC.

"German investigators believe a dispute over Ramadan meals led to a fire that gutted a shelter for 282 asylum seekers in the western city of Dusseldorf. They say a group of men who were not fasting had complained that their lunch portions were too small.

Two North African men, aged 26, have been arrested and charged with arson.

The hall was destroyed at a major Dusseldorf convention center close to the city's airport. Damage has been estimated at €10m ($11m; £8m).

The hall was acting as an accommodation hub for men mainly from Syria, Iraq, Afghanistan and North Africa."

What's going on in this country?

There's a man in Berlin, rumored to be Jewish, who might be able to explain this country to me. Should I drive to the capital?

What do you say, Opel, are you ready for a little ride?

Chapter 16

Gregor Gysi Loves Breakfast, Forget the Bundestag

At Café Einstein on Under den Linden I meet Gregor Gysi, a member of the Bundestag from Die Linke (the Left) party and the father figure of the left in Germany. Gregor orders black tea, I order black tea as well and, of course, Cola Light with ice and lemon.

What do you think about what happened in Dusseldorf? It seems, according to the news, that the refugees burnt their own home. Do you have any comment on it? I ask papa.
"I hope that it was a technical failure."
What do you mean by technical failure?
"Wrong electric wiring that had caused the fire. But there is also the possibility that it was an arson and then it has to be dealt with quickly and firmly."
Do you think that Angela Merkel acted well by not setting a limit on the number of refugees?
"It's good that she did not set a limit because a limit would be against our constitution and against international law, the Convention on Refugees. But this doesn't mean that her politics concerning the refugees is a good policy. I condemn what she's doing with Turkey. In the beginning, she gave a totally different impression; everybody thought that she wanted to open the borders and that she identified with the refugees. I think that what she wanted was that the refugee issue wouldn't take place on our border but other countries' borders. She hoped for a European solution and even opened the border for 48 hours (during a standoff between refugees and Hungarian forces). But now she tries to solve the problem through Turkey."
What happened to her that she changed her policy?
"Nothing changed. She didn't want to have the problem on the German border, but she wanted it rather be on the Turkish border."

Hello, Refugees!

In other words, she does not have a soft heart? She is not a mama--

"This I don't know, she might have a soft heart, but she also is under great pressure. So she opens the border and at the same time keeps the route closed."

And the German people clearly went along with it.

"She lost some people's sympathy when she opened the border, and they are the ones who moved to the AfD and such. But she lost much more sympathy when she made the deal with Turkey because everybody knows that we, the government, will be silent about human rights violations in Turkey."

But the German people seem to be okay with it. What happened to the German people?

In the beginning they were with her, and it looked as if all the Germans were so gracious, welcoming the refugees, but then she closes the border, from far away, and nobody goes to the street to demonstrate. What happened to the German people?

"Well, there were already people who went to the street, against the refugees, from the beginning. As for the others, they like to care for the refugees, but they won't go to the street to get more refugees."

Why not?

To answer this, Gregor comes up with an excuse that I'm not sure even he understands. But here goes: The political right called for a demonstration against Angela Merkel, and if the left demonstrated against Angela Merkel as well it would look as if the two of them had joined forces since the media would not differentiate between the two sides, and this is very bad.

Did you get it? If you didn't, don't worry. Not all people are built to understand German politics, either of the right or the left.

I think now it's time that I ask him the question I have asked zillion others. Why is it, I ask him, that Germany has taken more refugees than any other European country?

"Mere numbers don't mean much. Germany is far bigger than Liechtenstein or Luxemburg, and saying that we took in more refugees than these two countries doesn't mean anything.

Secondly, I am not against it at all, even if we did. Germany is the strongest European country, economically, and we certainly can accept more people."

And that's not all. "We always discuss 'refugees,' but we never discuss the reason behind the refugee issue. How much America, Britain or Germany are responsible for it," he says.

How so?

While he does not accuse Germany of participating in the Iraq War or the Libyan bombardments, he says that Germany did fight in Afghanistan. "They also killed. They bombarded. Children lost their lives, and German soldiers died; there was death on both sides."

According to Gregor, Germany also participates in the Syrian war. How so? He explains: "We make [reconnaissance] planes available for them, and pilots identify the targets for them so they can bomb more accurately."

Who's "them"?

"The USA, Great Britain, France, etc."

The main country responsible for the wars in the Middle East is the United States. Yet the Germans feel they have to take so many refugees while the United States has said that it would take in only 10,000 refugees this year.

"America is guilty of everything, but our media won't criticize America."

But still, how come the Americans don't feel responsible and the Germans feel responsible?

"Because the Americans have a much bigger country, and they mostly look inward, domestically, not thinking about foreign affairs, but Germany is dependent on other countries. And this makes a big difference."

Gregor's relationship to America is not as simple as it first sounds. As we keep talking, he explains to me more of his thoughts about America.

"I will tell you something. A famous German journalist, the late Roger Willemsen, interviewed Madonna once. After a quarter of an hour, Madonna asked him: 'How come that while talking with you I have the same feelings as I have while talking with my psychiatrist? He answered: 'The reason is that I'm European and we ask funny questions.' Madonna replied: 'That's right, my psychiatrist also is from Argentina!' This tells you something, everything. Such a reply you would never hear from anybody in Germany. Do you understand? But I like the Americans. I experienced things over there, which one wouldn't even think were possible.

I'll give you two examples:

A professor, a German professor, gave lectures in America. One day he asked the president of the university, 'Tell me: how come you've never asked me how old I am'? She replied, 'I am not an idiot. If I, your superior, asked you for your age this would have been 'age-discrimination,' and it would cost me a full-year salary.' I always say, when I tell this story, that I find those regulations quite wise, but in Germany such a thing is unthinkable."

How old are you?

"I am 68."

Gregor doesn't forget. He has to give another example. And he goes on:

"I was with an American senator the other day, and I said to him: 'Could you please explain to me the theatrics about the American healthcare reform? What's the problem? Why not have everybody pay for universal healthcare so that when your neighbor is sick, he will be medically treated? What's the big deal about it? His eyes opened wide, and he said: 'Why should the health of my shitty neighbor be of interest to me?' It's totally a different thinking in America. I've also noticed, for instance, that waiters are very kind and polite. But then I realized that they earn very little, and if they didn't get tips they would hardly survive. So they are polite and kind. Here in Berlin, forget it!"

When it comes to food, I prefer the German food much more than the American, but when it comes to service I prefer the American way much more!

"I have to tell you: I'd rather not talk about American food! I also will not talk about British food! But there are countries where you can have an outstanding dinner, like in France, Spain, Italy, China and so on. Still, what all of them don't know how to do, is breakfast. German breakfast is the best! Not dinner, breakfast!"

What do you have for breakfast?

His face shines, his eyes glow, his lips dance when he talks about his breakfast: "Oh, for breakfast I eat three small toasts, with something different on each one of them. For example, salami, Leberwurst with cheese, or ham – which I especially like. Then, being that I am a spicy lad, I put horseradish on the ham. Then I still bite on a cucumber and tomato. And if I have enough time, I also make myself a soft egg. In addition to all of that, of course, I have tea and orange juice. And no matter what time I have to start work, I get up quite early so that I could prepare my breakfast! Otherwise I'll be hungry all day."

What time do you get up?

"It depends. Most often I don't get home before midnight… If, for instance, I have to leave the house at 8:00 a.m., then I get up at 6:30. If I have to leave at 9:00, I get up at 7:30, and if I have to leave at 10:00 I get up at 8:30."

Do you like the German culture?

"Well yes, kind of. I always, for example, had difficulties with the term 'Heimat' (homeland). I couldn't handle it. But then, the other day I went to the forest with a forester, and he loved his piece of earth so much. He knew every tree, he knew each animal, and all of a sudden it all became clear to me: Heimat. It didn't have anything to do with nationalism, but it had everything to do with the feeling of 'home;' this is something that I can relate to. And I also have to tell you when I fell in love with the German government workers. I was on a committee the other day, and there were two men shouting at each other; you can't imagine! I was afraid that a fight would break out between them. It was terrible, I thought. I didn't have a clue what was going on between them. It got worse and worse by the minute and then, in the middle of all the shouting and the yelling a government employee came over to me and explained to me that the fight was about paragraph 212-14. I was sitting there, and I imagined how at the end of the day that man would go home and at dinner he would say to his wife: 'Shall I tell you what happened today at the job?' Isn't this something, aha? I admire that!"

Hello, Refugees!

Do you think that one day the Syrians will be like them?

"A Syrian official who behaves like a German? This is still hard to imagine."

You are a member of the Bundestag. Why is it that after Merkel did her deal with Erdogan no vote was taken in the Bundestag against it? Why didn't you try to pass a law against the deal?

Honestly, I don't know if there was, or there was not, a vote in the Bundestag about this deal, but I ask Gregor anyway. Let's see what he will say.

"We can't enact a law against it," he says. "We can only demand that the Bundestag decide to ask her to withdraw from that deal, and this is what we have demanded, but the majority didn't agree with us."

Was it put to the vote?

"I think so. Or maybe it is still in the committee; this could also be the case. Either it's still in committee or it was already voted on. I'll try to find out."

Gregor, I see, knows as much as I do about what's going on in the Bundestag. How come? I don't know, but maybe this has to do with the fact that we are both Jewish. I mean, I think so. I've heard that he's "half" Jewish. Let me ask him.

Gregor, are you half Jewish?

"No, I can't say that. It depends on how you calculate this. If you use the Nuremberg Race Laws then I am only 37.5% Jewish; if you use the Jewish laws, then I'm not Jewish at all because I didn't have a Jewish mother. My grandfather was Jewish. I do have Jewish ancestors..."

You have a wonderful sense of humor. Is that part of your Jewish inheritance?

"Could be. How could I endure being a member of the Bundestag without humor? This is my survival strategy!"

Where did you get this humor? Papa, Mama?

"My father, that's my Jewish part. I will not deny it. I'll tell you something: Israel's (late) President, Shimon Peres, invited all the Jewish deputies from all parliaments for the 60th anniversary of Israel. When the Israeli ambassador to Germany told him that

124

there were no Jews in the Bundestag, Peres said: 'But there must be some people there who have Jewish ancestors!' The ambassador replied: 'Yes!'"

And Gregor was promptly invited.

I like this man. Meeting him provides me with a breath of fresh air, a sweet and funny pause in the rough world of refugees and the Germans who host them.

In the heavenly factory that manufacturers human beings they don't make people like Gregor anymore. This man is a treasure.

•

Following the interview, I get myself a schnitzel – they know how to make schnitzels at Café Einstein on Under den Linden, let me tell you – and once I'm done I go for a walk on Unter den Linden, Berlin's Fifth Avenue.

I make my way to the Brandenburg Gate, one of Germany's most symbolic sites.

And there, right in front of it, a long, long poster is held high and it reads: STOP THE WAR AGAINST MIGRANTS.

Hello, Refugees!

This is a demonstration against blocking refugees from coming to Germany.

An African guy, holding a loudspeaker, says: "We want free movement. We are also human beings. We are not beasts."

A few feet away from them I spot an Arab sitting on a bench and staring at some fixed point in the distant void. I approach him in Arabic and a bond immediately forms between us. He is from Lebanon, he tells me. How is Lebanon? I ask him. Great and safe, he says. Is Hizballah great as well?

"Excellent. Praised be Allah."

Are you a refugee?

"No!"

How long are you in Germany?

"Two months."

What made you come here?

"I married a German woman."

Must be beautiful, isn't she? Do you have a picture of her?

Yes, he does.

He has her picture on his smartphone and he shows her photo to me.

A gorgeous-looking lady, no doubt.

She's no blonde, in case that's what you thought. She's an Arab, and she wears a hijab. What do you think of the refugees coming here? I ask him.

"Some are okay but some have come here just for money; I don't like it."

I advance about six hundred feet and I meet Rashid, a Kurd who lives in Germany for twenty-five years.

"Germany is where my body is," he says, "but my soul is far away, in Iraq."

Son of Islamic parents, Rashid is an atheist. Yet, he tells me, "this country is not my home."

He is angry.

Having the refugees here in Germany, Rashid argues patiently, will end up destroying them. German companies want young people, he says, because the Germans are getting older and have few children. The Germans will get the new blood, says Rashid, the blood of the dead Arabs. "Look at me. Twenty-five years here. But I'm no German, I'm Kurdish and my home, my real home, is far away. German culture is not my culture, and I miss mine. The Germans and the West say that they care about us, but they don't. If they did, would they be friendly with Saudi Arabia? Saudi Arabia is exactly like Daesh, why is it that they keep diplomatic relations with Saudi Arabia? The West is playing games. They don't care about Arabs, Kurds or Afghanis."

Strong words.

But there are people who see it differently. Amnesty International, for example, claims in its literature that worldwide "the vast majority of people (80%) would welcome refugees with open arms," while in Germany the figure is 96%. These people, individuals, have nothing to do with Saudi Arabia but they do care about Arabs, Kurds, and Afghanis. At least according to Amnesty International.

Let me visit Amnesty International and see who they are.

I go there.

Amnesty International's office in Berlin takes up a number of rooms on the fourth floor of an office building. The office is clean, spotless but it lacks warmth; it looks more like a nuclear laboratory than an office. "Human rights," I guess, does not necessarily mean human warmth.

So be it.

The charming thing in this place, I must say, is the toilet for the disabled; this is the biggest toilet of its kind that I've ever encountered so far in my life. Not that I see any disabled people here, and I don't know how many people, disabled or not, visit this place -- but I'm impressed.

The refugees, let me tell you, would love to have a toilet like this. But they are not Amnesty. Sorry.

Amnesty, I'm told, wants to have the gates of Germany – and in any other country anywhere – wide open to all asylum seekers, no matter how many there are.

No limits, period.

Hello, Refugees!

And so I sit down to have a talk with a lady whose job title is, if I got it correctly, Policy Officer for Asylum Law and Politics, to hear more about refugees and Amnesty.

Joining us are two employees from the press department. Why have they joined us? This becomes apparent only at the end of my talk with the lady: "Send us," one of them says to me, "what you write before you publish anything."

Not that the lade had told here anything that one could not find in Amnesty's publicly-available literature, but Amnesty unmistakably wants to make sure that I write what its people want me to write.

This bizarre demand doesn't smell like anything even remotely related to Freedom of Press, a freedom that Amnesty International loudly fight for having all over the globe, and so I won't write anything of what the lady told me.

That said, let me share with you what Amnesty International claims publicly: "Globally, 1 in 10 would let refugees stay in their home." In China, Amnesty International says, that figure is 46%. Yes, you read it right: about half the Chinese would welcome refugees into their homes.

Don't you love the Chinese?

I think I should try out some of the good people of the world, namely Germans. I'll walk into a home whose people I don't know and ask them to take in a few refugees. Let's see what will happen!

Chapter 17

Three Young Male Muslims are Coming to Live with You. Is it Okay?

I drive to Brandenburg.
Have you been to Brandenburg City?
If you have not, maybe it's time you pay a visit.
As I park Astra near the church – I love old churches, I'm not really sure why – I encounter a lovely man who tells me that he supports opening the gates of Germany for the refugees. Germany is a rich country, he argues, and why not help people in need? I tell him that I have a couple of refugees who are looking for a place to stay and that I'm looking for a nice German family to host them. Would he mind?
He wouldn't mind, he says, but I should ask his wife.
Let's go to her and ask her, I suggest.
And so we go.
Will his family be my Amnesty Family?
Let's see.

When his teenage daughter hears my idea, she starts laughing as if this was the funniest, most irrational idea she has ever encountered.
Happily, the house of this man and daughter is nearby, and in minutes we reach their place.
The wife is home, and so I talk to her.
I'm working with refugees, I tell her, and I'm looking for a family to house three refugees for two months. Will it be okay with you if I tell them to come here?
"How old are they?" she inquires.
One is nineteen, one is twenty, and one is twenty-five, I inform her. Her husband told me, I say to her, that they could stay in one of the rooms of the house, but that it depended on her. Two Syrians and one Afghani, I give her a bit more details.
"I have to meet them first," she says.
They are good people, I tell her, and they have been approved by the German government. No reason to worry.

She says again that she wants to meet them first.

But your husband agreed, I protest, and then I suggest that she and her husband talk about it between themselves and call me later.

"What's your organization?" she asks.

Help for Refugees, I answer, making up an honest-sounding name.

"From the United Nations?" she asks.

Yes, I confirm; delighted that she believes my tale. Will it be okay if I bring them in?

The daughter, who is scheduled to leave home this week, is tremendously enjoying this interesting turn of events that is unfolding in front of her eyes, says it's okay with her.

Is it okay with you as well? I ask the mom. Could I bring them in, the three Arabs, all Muslim?

Afghanis are not Arabs, but she doesn't know. "I have to meet them first," she tells me, "because of their food, their way of cooking…"

Don't worry; I calm her down. This month is Ramadan, and they don't eat anything on Ramadan. Thirty days they eat nothing, only at night. Can I send for them to come in?

"Are they men?"

Yes, all men. Three men. It will be good for all of you; I try to convince her. You'll learn Arabic!

"They speak Arabic?"

Yes.

"Only Arabic?"

They speak a little German too, but very little. Should I ask them to come in, so that you can see them?

"Yes."

Would you mind if they come with their suitcases already?

"With the suitcases??"

Yes. In case you like them—

"I don't know," she says, and then adds: "Let them first come without their suitcases."

I'm sure you'll like them! I insist.

"We'll cook and eat together," says the husband, trying to save his wife, "and then we'll see."

"Where do they live now?" the wife asks.

In Berlin, on the street.

The couple is a bit concerned about all this, feeling forced into a situation they would rather avoid.

Feeling pity for them, I tell them that it's all a hoax, and that I'm not from the UN.

What a relief!

Where am I to go from here? Should I fly to China and pretend to be a refugee?

Nope. I would rather stay in Germany for a while.

Nearby is the Brandenburg Concentration Camp Memorial site, also known as Brandenburg Euthanasia Center, and locally known as Gedenkstätte für die Opfer der Euthanasie-Morde. I'm told that I should pass by.

I go there.

I look at the exhibitions and read some of the available material. Here's an example:

"Beginning of January 1940, for the very first time in Germany, several NS functionaries and T4 employees killed a group of patients with carbon monoxide in the 'Old Prison' in Brandenburg. At the same time, a few patients were killed by lethal injection. By that, the decision fell on the method of killing by means of gas, which became the signature of the NS genocide of European Jews."

The "patients" referred herein were people suffering from mental illnesses.

And in that horrifying scientific experiment, 9,772 people lost their lives at this very place.

It was right here, where I am standing right now, that the system of gassing millions of people was first tried, tested and put into effect.

Many members of my family found their death by this method long before I was born. And if to trust the people that I meet on my journey through the land these days, that scientific breakthrough, so to speak, which resulted in the killing of millions of Jews and others in the last century, makes the Germans of today welcome more than a million Muslims.

•

I keep on driving. Destination: Magdeburg.

Why Magdeburg?

Years back I was told by some Germans that the city of Magdeburg was practically leveled to the ground during World War Two and rebuilt from scratch. It will be interesting, I say to myself, to see how Magdeburg of today deals with the issue of refugees, people whose cities are being wiped out these days.

I drive on and on, until I reach Magdeburg.

Much of the city, the locals supply me with more exact details, was destroyed during the British Royal Air Force bombing on January 16, 1945.

In recognition of that historical event, it is the custom of neo-Nazi groups to congregate in this city on January of every year and demonstrate against the Brits. This demonstration breeds another custom, by various anti-fascist groups (often known as Antifa), who demonstrate against the demonstrators.

Will be interesting to meet some Antifa activists and have them share with me their thoughts on refugees.

Thanks heaven, soon enough I get my wish.

I meet Angela and Ralf, together with their newest friend, the 26-year-old Ali, a refugee from Syria.

Angela, following the fine German tradition of being absolutely exact, explains to me that she's not Antifa ("anti-fascist") but Antira ("anti-racist"). Big, huge difference!

These two Germans are Amnesty think-alike folks. They believe that Germany should keep its gates wide open to all refugees of the world. They also tell me that so far Germany hasn't done anything special in regards to the refugees, that Germany is bad, and that the refugees are great. Ali, on the other hand, declares that Germany is the most welcoming of refugees, that Germans are great people and that the refugee camp he's living in is great and that the food served in the camp is outstanding.

Outstanding. Wow! First time I hear something like this.

Hello, Refugees!

You come from Syria, I say to Ali, and Syria has been in constant state of war with Israel for decades. Is that correct?

Yes, it's correct, Ali responds. And then he tells me that Syria, Lebanon, Jordan, Israel, and Palestine are actually one entity.

Well, however you slice it, to Syrians the state of Israel is the state of the enemy. What will you do or feel if you happen to meet a Jew right here in Germany?

Ali refuses to answer. He doesn't want to discuss politics, he says.

But before Ali gets the chance to elaborate on his reply, Ralf jumps in and bitterly complains against me. This question, he says, should not be asked. Why, the hell, am I bringing up the "Jew thing"? he demands to know.

The man is pissed off; he is boiling.

In general, Jews are not his cup of tea. The Christians of Magdeburg, he says, help the refugees. The Muslims of Magdeburg "really do big things" for the refugees, and atheists also help the refugees. In short: everybody helps the refugees except for – guess who? – the Jews of Magdeburg. As far as he knows, he hasn't seen one Jew helping out.

Why is it that an anti-fascist gets so upset at the mention of the "Jew" word?

Ask him.

I do, and he gets ever angrier with me.

But Ali is not angry, and he is ready to elaborate a bit. First off, he says, he's a refugee and he doesn't want to share his thoughts on this subject. His thoughts are his, and nowhere is it written that he has to share them with others.

Fine.

Only he doesn't stop there.

He has nothing against Jews, or Israelis, who live in Germany. These Jews, he argues, don't carry guns. But the Jews over there, in Israel, are a different story. They are "Zionists," he says, and there's no difference between them and Daesh.

Jews = ISIS.

Period.

Once he gets his papers done in this country, he reveals, he will share his thoughts about the Jews in public.

As if he hasn't by now.

What will he do if, by chance, he gets to meet an Israeli right here in Germany?

Well, he will excuse himself and leave. "It is my right not to talk to him," he says.

How do you know Arabic? he asks me.

I tell him the usual story – that my mother is Jordanian – and we get to spend a wonderful evening together.

I ask Angela, quietly, if what Ali told me before about his magnificent camp is true or not. Not true, she says; the camp is an awful place.

Who is telling me the truth and who is not? The easiest way to find out would be to visit the place.

Would you mind if I come to visit you tomorrow at the camp? I ask Ali.

No problem, he says, and he gives me the exact address.

An extraordinary evening, I say to myself, but it gets quite strange once I reach my hotel.

Angela calls me. What happened? Ali asked her to tell me that he doesn't want me to visit him at the camp. Why? Well, this is complex, and it takes me some time to find out from Angela. The short and sweet of it is this: Angela gave Ali my last name and he checked it on the internet.

What did he find? That I was born in Israel, and that I'm no Arab.

So, he doesn't want to see me because I'm Jewish? I ask Angela.

"I don't know. No. Yes."

These are three answers in five words. But she justifies him anyway, like Ralf.

Antifa/Antira folks, who are supposedly dedicating their lives to fight racism, see nothing wrong with people who will not meet Jews. Why? Anti-Semitism, I guess, does not count as racism. Jews, after all, are not human.

It is at this very moment that I can think of nothing else but Brandenburg.

In my hotel, the Plaza Hotel in Magdeburg, they sell interesting reading material in the bar, which include magazines to engage your mind while you sip your coffee or drink your beer. One of those magazines is called *aspekt*.

What is *aspekt*? *aspekt* is an economic magazine, priced at €3.50.

To take my mind off refugees, Germans, and Jews, I read this *aspekt*.

Interesting material, let me tell you.

Should I share with you what I read?

I read about extremely important financial facts, for example, the Jewish banking family of Rothschild. According to *aspekt*, the Rothschild family owns 165 central banks, including the Fed, meaning the United States Federal Reserve system. For the past 230 years, *aspekt* writes, the Rothschild family is in control of every central bank in the world, except for the central banks of North Korea and Cuba.

Ja.

This racist propaganda is available to you for a small fee at a normal hotel in today's Germany.

Welcome, refugees. Get the hell out of here, Jews.

•

May I share the following with you, news not included in *aspekt*?

Here is from Bloomberg's news:

"Germany's biggest news magazine *Der Spiegel* threw its hat into the Brexit ring with a special edition, thicker and cheaper than usual, adorned with an image of the Union Jack and the German plea 'Bitte geht nicht!' or 'Please don't go!'

The issue that hit newsstands on Saturday costs 2 pounds, rather than the usual 5.20, in Britain and features 23 extra pages to accommodate English translations of all articles pertaining to Brexit. In no uncertain terms, it tells British readers 'it's smarter to stay.'"

And there's more:

"'We can no longer convince the British to love the EU. It's too late for that,' *Spiegel* wrote in the cover story. 'But perhaps we should use this opportunity to mention how much the rest of Europe admires them. It's unbelievable that they don't seem to see how much they've shaped the continent, how much we value them here, how close we Germans feel to them -- that too is part of the story.'"

What's going on with my Germans, have they lost their last bit of honor?

In a few days the British will vote in a referendum known as Brexit, where the Brits will choose either Leave, meaning exit the EU, or Remain, to remain in the EU. The vote is too close to call and the Germans, quite a sizable amount of them, want Britain to stay in the EU. Some in the German media, obviously, are at the point of losing their mind, forgetting that media is not supposed to be a propaganda tool but a news reporting utility.

•

Speaking of Europe.

There's something very European going on these days, the Euro games.

Let me join the people, Syrian or German, who get a kick out of watching how the pros kick a ball.

Chapter 18

All Arabs are Welcome, But the Jews are Nazis

I get into my silver – yeah, in case I forgot to mention this important detail – Opel Astra the next day and drive to Hannover, in the north of Germany. I've never been to Hannover, so it's time I be there. The drive is wonderful. I stop here and there, there and here and enjoy every inch of this land. Germany, let me tell you, is a beautiful country.

I get to Hannover late in the day and go to the SwissLife Hall arena to watch European football, soccer.

No, no. The games don't take place in Hannover. The 2016 UEFA European Championship, popularly known as Euro 2016, is a month-long football competition and this year it takes place in France. So, what's going on in Hannover? Like in many other cities in Germany, the Euro games are shown on huge screens, making it possible for the masses to come and watch the games with many others. It's called "Public Viewing," and in places like Berlin, for example, there are huge screens on some streets, where thousands upon thousands congregate as one to cheer for the German team.

Why would people not watch the games in the comfort of their living room and instead struggle for a better view among the thousands of heads all around them?

There's a reason for it.

What is it? I'm not sure, but I think that Germans extract tons of pleasure by rubbing shoulders with a gazillion other Germans.

Public Viewing is also a fabulous place to wrap your body in a huge German flag and feel super protected. And many Germans do exactly this.

Will be interesting to know what the game watchers think of the refugees.

There are countless people in attendance, all with their eyes fixed on a huge screen.

137

Hello, Refugees!

Standing next to me is an Iranian-born guy, and I start talking with him. He is in Germany for seven years by now, and he says that he is well-integrated and that he loves Germany. Why do you love Germany? I ask him.

"Here I can make good money."

What do you think of the refugees?

"Let them spread around, distribute them in other countries; not in Germany."

Next, I meet a young German guy, dressed in the colors of the German flag. Are you proud to be a German? I ask him.

It's not that easy for him to answer this question. Why so? "People will say that I'm a Nazi," he says, if he were to say that he's proud of being German.

But are you proud?

"Yes, I am."

I'm proud of you, man!

I try to concentrate on the game, but it's close to impossible to see anything. They are too tall, my Germans, and their heads cover my viewing field.

I walk out of the arena.

Outside, next to something that looks like a bus stop, I meet two young men, one Turkish and the other Moroccan, and both are German citizens.

Do you support having refugees in Germany?

"Only the Syrians," says the Turkish guy. "They need help, but not the other refugees." What's the problem with the others?

The other guy responds: "They came here for money. And they are not good. They steal, they do drugs—"

How do you know that the ones who do drugs are not Syrians…?

"Good question. I don't."

The non-native and the non-white Germans don't carry the "history" baggage, and that's why, I think, they are not afraid to state their opinion, because nobody would call them Nazis.

I go to my hotel.

Near the entrance to the hotel I see three young people, all from Sweden, and we start schmoozing.

Proportionally speaking, they tell me, Sweden took in more refugees than any other country. Why did Sweden take in so many refugees? I ask them. Because the Swedes are the most humane of people, one of then says.

Swedes, another one of them tells me, care more than others about human rights and that's why they took in more than their fair share.

Swedish people, they go on to teach me, are the fiercest enemies of all the racists world over.

If I'm not mistaken, I say to them, the Swedish people are quite obsessed with the Arab-Israeli conflict. Why is that?

"Israel is a mini Nazi state," one of them answers and the others concur.

I tell them that I'm German and that as a German I'm very offended by their statement.

I shouldn't be, they tell me. The Jews, they say, should have never been allowed to live in what is today "Israel." They should have been directed to settle somewhere else.

Where?

Wherever.

"When a Palestinian kills a Jew," the oldest-looking of them says, "the Jews retaliate and kill one hundred Palestinians."

Constantine of Munich told me that the Israelis kill thirty-six Palestinians for every dead Jew, but here the number jumps to one hundred.

And as in Munich, this guy doesn't have more details. Still, the other Swedes agree with his one hundred figure.

They try to argue with me, but no matter what I say they stick to their belief that the Jews are Nazis. End of story.

How could these most humane of people be so anti-Semitic?

Again and again, I'm shocked to see European lovers of refugees who are at the same time pure racists.

•

Hello, Refugees!

A bird whispers in my ears that in Dortmund there is a refugee camp on the water, on a ship. This sounds classic, and I think I should see it.

Chapter 19

No Journalists, Please!

On the next day, I reach Dortmund's harbor.

For the first time during this journey I try to gain entry into a refugee camp the way most journalists do, meaning via the press department of the office in charge of the camp. In my case today, it would be the city of Dortmund. But this fails. No journalist is allowed to visit the ship, I'm told. Also, no interview is allowed with Caritas, the church-based organization that runs the camp, without the presence of a City of Dortmund's social worker – who, of course, is not available today. In other words: No way, Jose.

I have to make it my way, by befriending the refugees.

I utter an Arabic blessing here, another Arabic blessing there to refugees that I meet and I'm in.

I am in the dining room.

Three Iraqis sit at a table, a fasting Muslim and two eating Christians. Christians don't fast on Ramadan. I join them.

How's life in here? I ask them.

"Eating, sleeping. Every day. And nothing more."

There are 150 refugees on this ship that moves nowhere, and all are bored. All they do, they tell me, is Wuallah shi, meaning nothing.

We chat a bit more until a security man catches up with me. He demands that I leave.

Hello, Refugees!

On the way out an older Arab lady tells me that life's very good on the ship, that Germany is very good, that everything's very good, and that soon she will be going to the hospital for an operation. Hospital is very good too, she says, even though she has not been there yet. She says these words in broken English, so that the guards will hear her saying these kind words.

It's sad to watch and to listen.

I'm not the only one thinking that this is sad.

Yasser (not his real name) does too. And once I'm out of the ship, Yasser approaches me and asks if I'd like to hear the real truth.

Yes, I say to him.

"Let's go to the garden," he says.

The "garden" is a ten-minute walk away, where green trees grow.

Once we find a place to hide from any official who might see us, Yasser talks. First off, he tells me that "I will speak on behalf of all my friends."

I'm all ears.

"Most of the refugees on the ship have spent more than seven months doing nothing. Most people in the camp are still waiting for approval to stay in Germany, and nothing has been done."

When did you arrive in Germany?

"I came to Germany in September 2015."

Tell me about life on the ship.

"It's not home. You are forced to eat what they cook, if it's good or not, and you have to eat it when they give it. But this is not the problem. Did you know that on Saturday a man tried to throw himself outside? One of the refugees left the ship, went to the top of the opposite building and tried to jump, to commit suicide." He shows me a photo of the man on the roof about to jump, which he captured on his smartphone.

Why did he try to jump?

"He has a health problem, and he didn't get any treatment. He wanted to live in an apartment, not on a ship. He wanted to get an interview with the government to get his status approved, and he didn't get the interview. For months. This is the main problem: not getting the interview. As long as they don't get their status approved, refugees are not allowed to work, and they are not allowed to leave Dortmund."

How did the story end?

"Police came. They promised to give him an apartment and offered him proper treatment. They took him to the hospital and now he's back on the ship."

Yasser is from Yarmouk, a Palestinian refugee camp in Damascus.

Yasser tells me that even though he was born in Syria, he's actually from Palestine, from the city of Akko. Akko is in Israel proper, within the green line, an area that even Palestinian leaders say they recognize as Israel. But, still, Yasser sees himself as a son of Akko, a city he has never even been to. He is like Suleiman, the refugee I met at the dog hotel in the east, the guy with the snake.

And since Yasser is a refugee, a born refugee, Syrian authorities have never issued a passport for him. In other words: he is not a citizen, never was and never will be, but a "Palestinian refugee." People like him, in the thousands upon thousands, made Yarmouk their home. But horrible things happened in Yarmouk during the current war in Syria, he tells me.

What happened in Yarmouk, Yasser?

"Destroyed."

When?

"Three years ago."

Tell me the story.

"I was born in Yarmouk, a very quiet area. A special place for the Palestinian people."

What happened in Yarmouk?

"One day, in the afternoon, I heard a long, wild noise. Bombing. The opposition, I don't know their name, was fighting Basher el-Assad's forces in Yarmouk, for two hours, and the army of Assad sent aircraft to Yarmouk and they bombed the center of Yarmouk. Many injuries, many dead. At night the fighting increased, until next morning. I think it was exactly on the 17th of December, 2012. The opposition forces agreed to a ceasefire of one hour, to allow the people to leave. Most of them left. I also left, with my whole family, to another place in rural Damascus, where I got a poor house from a friend. I stayed there for one month. From there we went to a refugee camp inside Syria. My family is still there."

How long did you stay in that refugee camp?

"I stayed there until August 2015."

Which is when you decided to leave Syria, I guess. Why? What happened in August 2015?

"My life stopped completely. I am thirty-one years old. Previously I served in the Syrian army for two years, from 2005 to 2007. Basher el-Assad's army and the opposition forces that fight him, force guys like me to fight. I was sure that soon one group or another would force me to help them. But I didn't want to fight; I didn't want to kill people."

Let me understand something: You, a Palestinian, served in Basher el-Assad's army?

"No. Not in the regular army but in an army that is related to Assad's army. A special Palestinian unit."

Continue your story.

"I was afraid that I would be recruited again, in 2015, and I decided to leave."

It was hard for a Palestinian to leave Damascus, he says, because Assad wanted to be seen as protecting Palestinians and that's why he did not allow Palestinians to leave Damascus. Too many of them have left already, and if all of them would leave he wouldn't be able to present himself as the Protector of the Palestinians.

How did you manage to leave?

"With money. Everything is possible with money. I paid €1,000 to leave Damascus."

Did you bribe a government official?

"Sure!"

Where did you go?

"Turkey."

When you left, what was your destination?

"Germany or Sweden."

Why these two countries?

"I heard that the procedure to gain entry and to get a job was easy in Germany."

And why Sweden?

"I heard that Palestinians could get, very easily, Swedish citizenship."

In Germany, Yasser is classified as stateless "because I'm Palestinian." ("Ungeklärt" citizenship, in the official lingo.) His Syrian papers don't classify him as Syrian, and he doesn't even have a Syrian passport. The Syrians, he tells me, don't issue passports to Palestinians.

"My life is miserable. Israel occupies my land, and I suffer all my life."

I wonder how many more Akko or Akka people are in Germany these days.

But it's not only Akko that he must forget these days. His German papers specify that he cannot leave Dortmund. "I have friends in Mannheim and Frankfurt, but I'm not allowed to visit them. Why? Why?"

Life on the ship, he tells me before we depart, is not good. If he opens the window of his room or cabin, it stinks; if he keeps it closed, he can't breathe. There's an air conditioner, but it doesn't work all the time. He would prefer, I think, the dog hotel.

When it's time to say goodbye, he asks that I help him and then he leaves. He leaves first; we are not to be seen together.

He goes to his ship, and I go back to my Opel. My air conditioner works, and I drive on.

Dusseldorf is not far from here, and I want to see the burnt refugee camp.

Chapter 20

Journalists Get Free Breakfast and Ask No Questions

Driving in Dusseldorf, a strange image pops up in front of my eyes: an "inflated" unit, of which people walk in and out. I stop to take a closer look and soon realize that this is a refugee camp. Go figure. From the outside, this bizarre structure looks like a huge balloon, but inside it, there are many rooms, with many refugees. The security folks won't let me in, so I talk to the people who are presently outside; they tell me that it's very hot inside.

I move on. Gotta see the burnt camp. The only question is: Where the heck is it? If I remember correctly from the reports that I read about the incident, the camp was in the old convention center of Dusseldorf, possibly similar to that camp in Leipzig.

I drive around and around until I spot an official of the convention center who says that I must have a permit to approach the site, and that no photo taking is allowed.

But where exactly is the site? This she wouldn't reveal.

It takes me an additional half-an-hour of driving, trying this road and that, until I find the burnt camp.

While driving, I frequently stopped to ask locals for directions but they were not much help, as every second person guided me to a different road.

But finally, Opel Astra got me there.

I get out and stand to face the camp that was.

Oh boy, it looks awful! The place is burnt to the ground, with almost nothing left. There are some poles still standing, and some strange-looking ashen parts on the ground, but that's it.

This place, a burnt lot, reminds me of Syria.

It probably reminds the refugees of home.

I stick around for a few minutes, and then step back. I take a few shots of the place, the forbidden shots, and slowly depart.

Hello, Refugees!

•

The Interior Minister of NRW (Nordrhein-Westfalen, the most populous German state), Ralf Jäger, is holding a breakfast press conference today on the issue of refugees at the State Chancellery in Dusseldorf. Ralf is a member of the SPD, Germany's Social Democrats, and I want to meet SPD officials. In addition, and since he is a minister, I want to ask him about my encounter yesterday with the Dortmund officials who wouldn't allow journalists to meet refugees or camp managers.

I arrive late, almost at the end of the press conference, and there's not one seat available at the table. It's a big table, with food and drinks on it, but I can't help myself to a single bite. And so, instead, I just examine the table with my eyes. The minister sits at the middle of the table, flanked by two aides – I don't know their official titles – and the journalists sit around them.

In a normally functioning democracy, the minister will be grilled by the media once the Q&A session starts. Will be interesting to see what will happen here.

Meantime I watch my surrounding. If I can't fill my mouth with food, let me feed my eyes with images. I look at the food on the table. German breakfast. It reminds me of Gregor Gysi, the man in love with German breakfast.

There are croissants on the table, half slices of bread with different toppings, such as salami and cheese; others have a slice of egg on top of the topping as well. There is also yogurt in shiny glasses, apple juice, mineral water, tea, and coffee.

Doesn't look bad.

And soon enough, the Q&A starts.

The journalists, well fed by now, ask for more detailed information of what they just have heard but none asks any probing questions. They like the minister's company, and they won't challenge him. Ralf cracks a joke or something like a joke, and the journalists laugh. I start to have the feeling that this is a family reunion. Turkish president Recep Tayyip Erdogan, I believe, would feel comfortable with these journalists. Recep, as is well known, likes reporters who admire him; the ones he doesn't like are writing their reports in dark prison cells.

These journalists, let me assure you, will get along with Recep just fine.

Disrupting this happy shmhappy party between minister and journalists I raise my hand and ask His Honor to tell me if what I experienced with the Dortmund officials is a policy that he instituted? The person sitting next to His Highness, an official, interjects and tells me that since this press conference deals mainly with North African refugees, I should wait until after the press conference, a time when the minister will be available to answer my question.

Good. I can wait.

There's an empty seat by the wall behind the back of the minister, which just became available, and I move to take possession of it.

I look at His Honor, Ralf.

The minister is dressed extremely well and from where I sit, having an extraordinary and an extremely-close back view, I see what no other journalist here can. Ralf's jacket, with shoulders straight in 45 degrees, gives the impression that he is a statue, not a breathing being. It's damn perfect! His haircut, ever so exact, would win a Guinness prize; no hair is longer, or shorter than it should be. Photoshop couldn't do better.

Under the table, from my back view, I see His Honor constantly shaking and moving his feet. The man must be extremely nervous. I wonder why.

Sitting near me are the minister's secretaries, three of them. Each, at his or her turn, gets up now and then and approach the Honor to whisper a word or a sentence in the statue's ears.

Time passes, as it naturally does everywhere, and the conference ends. And now, I'm told, I could talk to the minister.

Well, not so fast.

His presspersons, two of them, plus a manager, approach me. What would I like to know? they ask. Perhaps they could help.

I tell them of what I experienced in Dortmund, in the state of NRW, and say that I would like to have a direct quote from the minister on this.

They tell me that this has nothing to do with the minister. There are four thousand refugee camps in NRW, but only one hundred of them are under the control of the ministry, meaning of the state. All others used to be under the control of the ministry but they were given to the cities, and they are the ones who make the rules. Nothing to do with the minister or the ministry. I ask them if the state has certain guidelines which it requires the cities to follow before they get control of it since it seems to me that the issue of freedom of the press is a principle that the state should require the cities to observe.

They look at me.

We talk some more, and they tell me that they would be, of course, ready to have me visit any of the camps under their direct control.

No, they have nothing they can offer in Dusseldorf. Am I interested in any other city?

Yes, I say. I'm driving around in the NRW and would be glad to visit a camp or two.

They could get me into a camp in Bonn, they say. I accept their offer.

They have my contact information, and they will notify me about the camp that I'll be able to visit.

Good.

But, of course, I still want to talk to the minister, if they don't mind. I have been promised, in front of everybody, that His Honor would give me an audience, and I want it.

Yes, of course; they say. "Now you can talk to the minister."

We go to another room, where the minister is at the moment, but His Honor refuses to talk with me.

I grab a bite, leave the building, get into my silver car and drive to find the gold in Bonn.

Chapter 21

Enemy of the People

So, what do you think? Do you think that anyone associated with His Honor, Minister Ralf Jäger, had contacted me?
Well, no one.

It is time, I believe, that I get myself acquainted with a man that German journalists would love to watch being hung on the tallest trees while they're feasting at their Feed Me press conferences.
The name of the man is Akif Pirinçci, a Bonn resident.
Do you know Akif? Akif is an author, an international bestselling author who has written a number of thrillers whose protagonists are cats. Sounds pretty interesting, doesn't it? But there are more interesting things about Akif than cats.
What are they? I'll tell you.
Not long ago he said something in public and the German media, many of them, quoted him. And it sounded quite horrible.
What did he say?
According to the media, this is what Akif said at a Pegida demonstration in Dresden late last year when speaking of refugees: "Unfortunately, the concentration camps are out of order at the moment."
When this became public, Akif's publisher, Random House, canceled all contracts with him and stopped selling his books. Additionally, Amazon in Germany, and essentially all German bookstores, have done the same. Not only that: Volker Beck, the Green Party MP I met in Berlin about a month ago, filed charges against Akif for "Incitement to Hatred."
Did Akif indeed say what the media claims he said?

Akif lives in a fine Bonn neighborhood, and it doesn't take much imagination to know where on the block he lives. I figure it out quite fast. Will you too? Come over here and look. Look at the entrance to that house over there, about five houses up the road. Do you see it? It's a nice-looking multi-level house, but the steps at the entrance seem to have been damaged by force. Don't you think? Now, look at the gorgeous entrance door. You see it? Somebody, or some people, splashed black and pink paint on the door and the front wall.

Yeah.

Who did it and when?

Now look above the door, a floor above, and there you can see a man standing on the balcony looking out.

Who is that man?

Akif, of course.

I advance to the house, and he leaves the balcony.

He walks his way downstairs, I believe.

And indeed so.

Akif, a short man next to a big and dirty door, says Hello.

What happened here, man?

Two months ago, he tells me while welcoming me in, an Antifa group splashed the entrance to his abode with this ugly black and pink, and damaged the steps as well.

Well, that's life.

Hello, Refugees!

I enter his beautiful home which he bought, he tells me, with the money he earned from selling his books. How many books did you sell so far? "By now, five million books in Germany." And then there are many translations. "My books have been translated into almost all languages, but not to Hebrew..."

Why not?

"I don't know."

The man has read about me, I guess, and he knows that I'm Jewish.

So be it.

We sit down, and I tell him that I have a number of questions for him. Would he mind answering them and would he mind if I publish his responses and write about him?

"You can write whatever you want about me, true or false," he responds.

This means that I can leave right now and write whatever comes to my mind, but I stay.

This man is funny, and I want to hear what he has to say.

What exactly did you say at the Pegida demonstration in Dresden? I ask him.

"I was quoting from my book, which was not yet published at the time."

The man, if what he says is true, was not giving a speech but a book reading.

And before I even can verify what he says by whatever means, Akif points to a book on his table. The name of the book is Umvolkung, published by Antaios, Götz Kubitschek's publishing company. Kubitschek, you see, is Akif's only publisher now; no one else would publish him.

Akif opens the book and starts reading from it.

It's a story about a CDU politician who said to someone that, "If you don't like it (having the refugees here), you have the option, and the right, to leave the country." And it was to this response that Akif quipped with his pen: "There are some other options but, unfortunately, the concentration camps are out of order at the moment."

In other words, the "concentration camp" reference was nothing but a satirical comment about the person who doesn't want the refugees, giving that person another option, which doesn't exist, in addition to just leaving the country.

In short: whoever quoted Akif, didn't bother to check the context.

Not that Akif is pro-refugees, mind you; he is not. In his speech, he attacked the Muslim world and spoke quite lowly of Muslims in general, something he had done in the past as well. You and I might not condone his words, but I think that he has the right to say them. Had he used the same words about Jews, I would grant him the same right, despite the fact that I'm Jewish. Hey, better to know what people think about me than spend my days with "liberals" who tell me that they love me but in reality can't stand me and all other Jews.

Be that as it may, what did him in was the line about concentration camps, a line taken out of context and reinterpreted to give the impression that Akif had called to reopen the concentration camps, and this time around for the refugees.

"If anybody says such a thing seriously," Akif tells me, "that person is mentally sick."

But it doesn't matter what he really thinks.

"On the next day," Akif tells me, "my publisher, Random House – with whom I had a contract for €400,000, as an advance for three new books – broke their contract with me."

Is that legal?

"They said to me that they could do this to anyone who says blasphemous words, even a janitor would lose his job for uttering blasphemous words."

I hear him out, and I say to myself: If what he tells me is true, and the German media has indeed been lying through their noses, why isn't he suing them?

And so I ask him why he didn't sue the media.

"I sued twenty-eight papers, TV, and other media," he replies, "for what they quoted in my name, for changing my words. And all of them, all twenty-eight of them, put it in writing that they recognized that they were at fault, and they signed a legal document in which they obligated themselves to pay €250,000 for every such occurrence in the future."

Did you make their signed document public?

"Yes, on my homepage and on Facebook."

Can you show me a copy of what they signed (officially called "Unterlassungserklärung") to your lawyer?

He emails me a letter from his lawyer, which lists the media companies that signed the agreement. They include the following: *Die Zeit,* NDR, *Hannoversche Allgemeine, Leipziger Volkszeitung, Kieler Nachrichten, Südwest-Presse,* and *Schwäbisches Tagblatt.* In the letter the lawyer adds that ZDF's (the public broadcasting network) signature is forthcoming.

Would you send me an example of the agreement signed by the media?

Yes, he says, and he sends me one such agreement, signed in a Hamburg court, with the newspaper *Frankfurter Rundschau.*

This was never made public?

"No."

Why not?

The media in Germany is a "lying media," he says, and gives me an example of what he, and many on the right, call "Lying Media."

"Beginning of last year *Die Zeit* wrote a very big article, stating that 85% of refugees, about 100,000 at the time, had higher education. A very big article. Now I was asking myself: How did the author of this article come up with such a number? Why not 83% or 86%?

There are two possibilities for how he came up with such a number:

1. He called the immigration office and asked: 'How many of the asylum seekers have higher education?' and they said: '85%.' But this is impossible because this is like saying that even though many of the 100,000 who came to Germany at that time did not have their ID's and passports, they still had their academic papers...

2. The author went to the street and made a representative study, which would be 2,000 people. So, when he walked on the street and saw a veiled woman or an Arabic-looking man he asked them if they had a diploma, and they reached into their pockets, took out

155

their diplomas, and showed him something in Arabic, and this author then went to a translator to get it in German. This is possible but not probable..."

(It will proper to note here that the agreement between Akif and the media was made public by some news organizations, such as *Die Welt*, but many details of the agreement were not included.)

Akif reminds me of Gregor Gysi. Both are short, both are older, both like to tell stories, and both have a funny bone. Only that Gregor is left, very left, and Akif is right, very right.

But he can be serious as well.

"A journalist has to be neutral," Akif says to me, "and write facts, facts that he can prove. But this is not the case in Germany. What does the German journalist do? Because he is a criminal ideologist, Green-contaminated, he is on a mission to infuse fucking multi-culturalism into the readers' minds."

Akif doesn't think much of the press, but he thinks much less of the refugees. "As we now know," he says, "30% of the refugees are analphabets, another 50% are functional analphabets, meaning they can read but they don't understand what they're reading. Then there's the rest, the 20%, and they are only partially educated."

How did Akif get these numbers? Allah knows.

Akif does not stop criticizing. He has spoken badly of the press, badly of the refugees, and now he moves to speak badly of himself: "I drink a bottle and a half of wine a day, and I smoke 70 cigarettes a day...and I also drink schnapps."

Smoking one cigarette after another, like the late German Chancellor Helmut Schmidt used to do, Akif soon comes back to the issue of the "lying press."

"On New Year's Eve 2016, at the Cologne Cathedral, women were attacked by thousand to thousand-five-hundred refugees, who surrounded them, raped them and robbed them. In the beginning, the media was quiet. ZDF, for example, admitted to have withheld information about what had happened on New Year's Eve for four days. When the story finally broke out, the German press, in unanimity, said that these crimes can potentially happen when men come together in one place, like in Oktoberfest or in the Cologne Carnival, and that what happened in Cologne on New Year's Eve was not unique to Middle Eastern men."

And now he analyzes it:

"This would mean that during the Cologne Carnival 1,500 men usually come together, surround women, and say: 'Let's rape them!' Same thing in Oktoberfest: 1,500 men rape women on a normal basis. I have never heard of it! Last Oktoberfest, with seven million participants, the police registered four attempted or committed rapes. That's it."

My Turkish-turned-German man is pissed off.

"Following the event in Cologne, the Green Party called for a demonstration in front of the Cathedral against what they termed 'male violence.' What does this mean? Are you violent?"

Time to change the topic.

Is Amazon really not selling your books?

"Not directly, only through a third party. The e-books are not available at all. I have eight novels about cats, and they are not available for sale. Amazon sells KKK (Ku Klux Klan) books. They also sell seventy versions of *Mein Kampf*, a book that calls to exterminate Jews. But not my cat books. Those Amazon people are shit-faced ass fuckers. To hell with them!"

The one media organization that practiced proper journalism, he says, was *Der Spiegel*. "They published my words in full, and in context," he explains.

And he goes on: "My tool as an author is freedom of speech, and this is being denied me. My own publisher sent letters to Thalia bookstores (one of Germany's largest bookstore chains) saying that Akif doesn't exist. I don't think that during the Nazi time people behaved like this. They might have said that the book by this or that author was forbidden, but they did not say that Thomas Mann didn't exist."

Tell me, Akif, what are you? Are you Christian, Muslim, atheist, Jewish?

"I am a Satan worshipper. I believe in the evil in the world. That's the only god that's left."

So, atheist?

"Of course."

Your parents?

"Traditional Muslims."

Who are his friends? you may ask, but that's a moot question. And if you do ask this of Akif, this is what he'll say: "I don't have friends. Only young women. I can show you the photos of the women I've slept with. I take photos so that people will believe me."

Let me see the pix!

Akif shows me a photo of a 19-year old blonde on his smartphone which, he says, he slept with five times on the first night, adding: "I don't want to brag..."

Kossai showed me a destroyed home on his smartphone, Yasser showed me a suicidal man on his smartphone, and Akif shows me a young babe on his smartphone.

To each his story, and Akif has his.

Yep. Akif loves women. Too much. Especially those of the paler skin.

"I love white women. I love women who look as if they would break any moment because of lack of blood. Maybe this is the Oriental's conquering instinct..."

Akif now reminds of the Lebanese refugee, Yunis, who spends his days crying, begging Allah to find him a blonde German beauty to marry.

Akif, smartphone in hand, proceeds to show me a red-haired, and a black-haired, and another blonde -- all white-skinned ladies, his dream babes.

If Akif ever entered a refugee camp, a thought comes to me, he would certainly feel home there with the people. He looks like them, he thinks like them, he dreams like them. He is them. The only difference between them and him is that he made it here, that he integrated into this society and writes best sellers in the German language.

Well, until recently.

We walk up to the second floor of his richly and tastefully decorated house, and stop for a second at his bedroom. "Here's where you make love to the 19-year-olds? I ask him. "Yes," he says, gleefully. We pass by his bathtub. "Here's where you take a shower with the ladies?" I ask him. "We play here! You understand?" he answers, and his mischievous eyes shine.

Akif, I slowly learn, will say anything for the mere pleasure of it.

It is time we leave the house and go out to eat.

Not an easy task, if you are Akif.

We walk a couple of steps, everything looks good, but then it's not. A young man passes by us and starts bullying him, as if Akif were a dirty, wild dog.

This is probably, I say to myself, what the classmates of Frauke Petry's children did to them.

Akif is hurt, and upset. But the bully wouldn't stop.

We continue to walk.

It was sad to watch.

But Akif tries to make light of it.

"A writer has a boring life, sitting at the desk all the time and writing," he says to me, but his life is not boring, not at all, can't I see?

His attempt to present the hatred of the people toward him in a positive light is something that I don't buy. He is hurt, deeply hurt, but it's hard for him to admit it. The other day, he tells me, somebody emptied a bottle of Coke over his head as he walked on the street.

We keep walking until we arrive at the restaurant.

We sit down.

This is an important detail, by the way. Some restaurants, Akif tells me, have announced that they would not serve him if and when he showed up at their establishments. But this restaurant, lucky him, will serve him food for money.

Great.

We chat, and we eat as well.

Akif tells jokes, many of them, and talks again about how much he's attracted to white-skinned females. The whiter their skin is, the more he's into them.

Akif is a small Turkish boy who dreams to have a white lady, he shares with me.

In between his jokes and stories, this dish and that, we go out to have a smoke.

Not an easy task if your name is Akif.

An older couple, who leave the restaurant at the same time, stop to look at Akif. No, they are not friends, and Akif has never met them before. The old man, well-dressed, gets busy taunting Akif. Just like the young man did before.

Young and old Germans have nothing better to do than to hurt Akif.

Akif. Enemy of the People.

Yes. He is, lo and behold, the Enemy of the People.

I watch what unfolds in front of my eyes, and I think: Give people the chance to hurt and humiliate, tell them that cruelty is a virtue, and they will turn into animals. Adolf Hitler tried this formula last century, and it worked. Today, self-declared humanists are trying it as well, and it still works.

A playwright should write Akif's story, a Turkish man in a ruthless Germany.

The older couple leaves, and we smoke and talk.

It is time for Akif to tell me his real German story.

He was a boy when he came to Germany with his parents. His father was a "guest worker," one of the myriads of Turks who at that time came to Germany to do the work which the average German didn't want to do. But before coming to Germany, his father had to go through a test to see if this country indeed wanted him. The test was pretty simple: The father was told to stand naked for an inspection. Once in the nude, German doctors examined his naked body to make sure that all his parts were in place and functioning.

Pretty much like the Nazi doctors did in the concentration camps, Akif reminds me.

The way Dr. Josef Mengele selected people.

What a humiliation.

Akif, the artist that he is, pokes fun at everybody. The Muslims are idiots, the Germans are Nazis, and he's busy making love to young white-skinned Germans in his bathtub.

Akif is a Turk who embraced Germans, but the Germans spit in his face.

I tell him this, and it hurts him.

Moments later, Akif takes a long drag from his cigarette, looks me straight in the eye and says: "Soon you and I will get old. Our bones will ache, our organs will stop functioning, and we will fly up. You to God, and I to Allah."

He touches me. Deeply.

Akif, if you didn't know, is an artist. An author. A free spirit.

A boycotted author.

In the old days they burned books in this country; these days they erase authors.

Luckily for Akif, the crematoriums don't function momentarily.

What makes people so righteous? I ask myself. What drives them into humiliating those who don't agree with them?

You tell me.

I bid Akif goodbye and am left to my own thoughts.

What's his crime? He makes fun of Islam. He, the Turkish boy who became a German citizen, is poking fun at the religion of his parents, and he ridicules his own culture and people.

I know people like him. White Germans who poke fun at Christianity, the religion of their parents, and they ridicule their own culture and people – and at times deliver hate speeches against Christians, similar or worse than what Akif does. They are, as you and I know, the artists of Germany, its writers, and its cultural elite. They, the whites, have the right to do this and they are put on pedestals for doing so. Akif has no right to do this. Because he's a Turk. Because he is of a darker skin. Because his parents were Muslim.

Yeah.

I keep thinking, and what I come up with is not pretty.

Nope.

If Akif's writings are not to be sold in Germany due to his beliefs, whatever they may be, why are the operas of Richard Wagner, the Nazis' favorite, heard on the most prominent of German stages to this day?

Richard was a Nazi, but this is forgiven.

Richard Wagner was no brown man.

Simply stated, in today's Germany the whites have rights that the non-whites don't have. This is how the politically correct people think. They are, to put it succinctly, fucking racists. What they allow themselves, they will never allow the other, the stranger, the outsider.

Beware, you of Syria, Libya, and North Africa: Your day will come soon and, like Akif, you'll learn that none here will love you unless you stay at the bottom.

Akif is the most politically incorrect man I have ever met. A drinker, a smoker, a man of the flesh, and a man who is free.

The refugee issue in Germany, with all its pros and cons, are embodied in this one person, in Akif. And in more ways than one he is the refugee, not from Syria but Turkey, and in more ways than one he is German, the German who dedicates his time toiling for a better Germany, the way he believes it. Akif is a foreigner who integrated all too well in this country, a dark-skinned man who dreams of the white-skinned woman. And for this he will never be forgiven.

He is the unwanted.

What do the people of this country want? Britain. The news organization where I serve as a columnist, *Zeit Online*, inserted an image of a red heart and Britain's flag next to its title, the *Zeit Online* logo.

Zeit Online Loves Britain, meaning: Please Brits, please vote Remain!

Whatever happened to journalism?

In Frankfurt, not far from here, a man who would like to see Akif behind bars is attending a conference called Fourth Israel Congress. I think I should meet him.

Go, Astra, go! The winds blow yonder!

Chapter 22

It All Started with The Jews

Volker Beck is on one of the panels at the conference in Frankfurt. As fate would have it, I am a speaker at that very conference. Naturally, we meet at the VIP room, and I ask Volker to sit down with me for an interview.

Initially, he resists it. I was unfair, he says, at the queer event in Berlin a few weeks ago. He feels that I was making fun of the event, because I asked him to show me the Arab queers and he could point to just one queer. The event, he says, was not about refugee queers but queers in general, and so it doesn't matter how many refugee queers showed up or not.

I'm not going to argue this with him. Maybe the Greens have a queer party every year or every decade, but the way they advertised the event left no other impression than the one I had.

Hey, that's why I came.

But who cares? Let him have it the way he wants. I want to talk to him about refugees and Germans, I tell him, not about queers of any kind.

This he agrees to do, and so we sit down for a little talk.

I am curious as to why he's attending this Jewish event, and he tells me that in addition to his other roles in the Bundestag he is also the "President of the German-Israeli Friendship Group of the German Bundestag, a non-partisan group." Interesting. But I want to talk about refugees, not Jews.

Are you supporting Angela Merkel's policy, at least the policy that she used to have, of keeping Germany's gates open to refugees without setting any limit? I ask him.

"This is not a political issue," he replies. According to the Geneva Convention and our Constitution, if a refugee reaches our country he has the right to a procedure that will clarify if he's really persecuted, and therefore entitled to protection under the Geneva Convention. If he's not entitled, he has to go back. "

No limits?

Hello, Refugees!

"Without limits. The Geneva Convention for Refugees was established after the Second World War as a result of what happened with Jewish refugees who reached the borders [of different countries] and everybody said, 'We have reached our limit, you have to go back.' Think of the St. Louis ship, which was sent back from Cuba, US and Canada and many of the people who were on the ship ended their lives in Auschwitz. Think of the Évian Conference.

These events were the reason for the creation of the Geneva Convention for Refugees, that something like that will never happen again."

No matter what's the topic, I see, "Jews" sneak in.

If you wonder about Volker's references to the historical events, here they are in short:

■ The Évian Conference convened in July 1938 in France for the purpose of dealing with the issue of Jewish refugees who had fled for their lives from Nazi Germany. Only two of the thirty-two countries in attendance agreed to increase the number of Jews allowed into their territories. Not one European country agreed, and neither did the United States.

■ In May of 1939 the transatlantic liner St. Louis, carrying close to one thousand refugees, mostly Jews, sailed from Germany to Cuba, where they were initially guaranteed entry, but were consequently denied that entry. Their attempt to enter the USA and Canada also failed, and the ship sailed back to the European Continent. About one-quarter of its passengers eventually perished in Nazi death camps.

No other country of those who are signatories to the Geneva Convention, I say to him, observes the Geneva Convention – except for Germany. Why?

This is no longer the case, he replies. Now Germany is part of the "deal with Turkey, and we behave the same way" as the others. In others words: The German government flip-flopped and is no longer keeping the No Limit policy.

Which is, of course, true.

Why this flip-flop of German policies? I ask him.

"This question you have to ask Mrs. Merkel, I'm not her spokesman."

Why didn't your party, or Die Linke, put the Turkey deal to the vote in the Bundestag?

"We put it to a vote several times. We put forward resolutions which condemned the way we were working together with Turkey, with Erdogan."

I'm not sure I get it, so I ask again: Did you put it for a vote?

"Several times; we had drafts, and we also decided."

Was there a vote?

"Naturally."

I don't get the "several times" part of his reply, so I ask: When was the last time that you voted on it?

"Ask my chief; he's responsible—"

I have no idea who he's talking about, and I'm not going to any chief. Did you vote on it?
I ask him.

"Yes, several times. I spoke on this issue, and we are actually discussing several laws, for instance, the Integration Law."

I mean a vote against the deal with Erdogan. Did the deal go for a vote in the Bundestag?

"If you let me finish my sentence, you'll have the answer. In the new Integration Law of the government, the deal with Turkey will be introduced in the Migration Law, and we are criticizing this, and we'll vote against it."

So, it was not put to the vote yet?

German politicians are not an easy bunch. In reply to my question, he goes on and on and on, complicating the issue ever more. I try to make it simple for him: Was this part of the agreement, the part which calls for Turkey to stop refugees from crossing into Europe, was this part put to the vote in the Bundestag? Yes or no?

The answer is: No.

Why not? Because "this is an agreement between the European Union and Turkey, not between the Federal Republic of Germany and Turkey."

Same as with Gregor Gysi and Frauke Petry, it's hard to get a quick response from German politicians if they voted or not on this or that particular issue.

There is another Geneva Convention, the 1949 Fourth Geneva Convention, which declares that an "Occupying Power shall not deport or transfer parts of its own civilian population into the territory it occupies." And many Europeans, the same ones who fail to comply with a Geneva Convention that applies to them, still accuse Israel of not complying with the 1949 Convention. So I ask Volker, the Israel-friendly German, if Europeans can point any finger at Israel for not observing a Convention when Europe itself doesn't care much about Conventions? His reply: "I don't think that if somebody makes a mistake, somebody else has the right to make a mistake" as well.

But can you preach to others to do what you don't?

"Preaching is something for religious people. I think that everybody has to accept criticism. If you say somebody is allowed to criticize somebody else only if he's perfect, then you wouldn't have any criticism."

I admire Volker. For the life of me, I couldn't have a sentence like this pass through my lips, but he can.

•

Not only Merkel flip-flops. According to polls I've seen, the German people, in general, have changed their mind on the issue of refugees as well. They loved the refugees before Sylvester (New Year's Eve), welcoming them with teddy bears, but lost their love after Sylvester, when hundreds of women were beaten and sexually abused in Cologne by men who like to play with teddy bears.

Who should know best what really happened in Cologne on Sylvester night? The mayor of Cologne, I'd assume. Let's meet her.

I play with my Opel and drive to Cologne.

Chapter 23

They Threw Fireworks at the Church and Then They Raped the White Girls

Her Honor Henriette Reker is the Mayor of Cologne.

A day before the mayoral elections last year Henriette, a staunch pro-refugee person, was stabbed with a knife by a man with an aversion to refugees. She was elected into office while fighting for her life at the hospital, and as far as I know she fully recovered by now.

When I come to visit Her Honor, it is World Refugee Day.

Have you not heard of this day? There is Mother's Day, Secretary's Day, Father's Day, Earth Day, Independence Day and now also World Refugee Day.

Henriette is not alone in her office; her pressperson is also attending.

When did you know, when did the police know, when did the media know what happened on Sylvester night? I ask Her Honor.

"I knew that criminal acts took place on January 2, but not to the extent that had become known later."

Did you know, on January 2, that refugees were involved?

"No."

When did you know for the first time that refugees were involved?

"This I don't know even now. This kind of information I only read in the papers."

As far as you know: When did the German media, not social media, first report that refugees were the attackers?

"Many people who were present at the plaza (between the Cologne Cathedral and the central train station) appear to have been people from North Africa, but for me, this is not enough to conclude that the refugees were the ones who attacked the women."

Hello, Refugees!

Let me ask you this: Is it correct to say that information was given to the media about suspicions that the attackers were refugees, but the media withheld this information for a few days?

"I don't know. I can't answer this."

Do you remember when was the first time that you heard that refugees might have been involved in the attacks?

"I have to check this. I don't remember at the moment."

I assume that some crimes happen every Sylvester night. What was the average crime rate on Sylvester in the years before? How many complaints did the police receive last year?

The pressperson says that on the average there are about twenty complaints, fourteen to fifteen of them of sexual nature.

But Her Honor says: "I don't know."

Did you ask the police for a comparison study with past years?

No, she did not. What she knows is this: This year's Sylvester saw about 1,200 complaints, of which about 500 of them were of sexual nature.

Okay. Whatever the average numbers were for the past years, they were never even close to what happened this year. Something happened this year that did not happen before.

"Yes, definitely."

Can we assume that this year there were many more refugees in attendance than the years before?

"I can't say that the reason behind what happened this Sylvester is that there were more refugees at the plaza. What I can say is that this time around there were more criminals."

Can we say that this year there were more North Africans than in the other years?

"We can say that this year there were more people who looked like North Africans; this is what we can say."

Then she 'improves' her statement: "What we really can say is this: This year there were more men of a different culture, with different views about women than we have in our culture."

So, can we then say that the people who look like North Africans were the ones who committed those acts?

"Yes, we can." She pauses for a second, and then adds: "This is just a speculation."

It's hard to be a German these days. You have to think ten times before you say anything because otherwise, people will treat you the way they treat Akif. It is amazing how she struggles to be politically correct as she's correcting herself, again and again.

I try to get her to feel more comfortable. I say to her: I was in New York when all that happened. I watched how the story was unfolding in social media but not on the mainstream media. It seemed that the German media did not tell the story until practically being forced to tell it because the story came out via other channels. When did you know about the speculation that North Africans were the attackers?

"I get my information not from the papers but the police. First time I heard this, it was on Tuesday morning, January 5, when I was told of it by the police chief."

On the same day, by the way, the police chief, Wolfgang Albers, stood before reporters and told them that the police knew nothing about the identity of the attackers. Three days later he was forced out of office into early retirement by Ralf Jäger, the man who played a little game with me a few days ago in Dusseldorf.

What a small world.

The truth is that the identity of the attackers was reported immediately on social media, and I think that I should go to the plaza and try to cull information from some people there.

I'll do it tomorrow, not today. Today, meaning this evening, Her Honor invites me to attend "China Event." I have no clue what it is, but I'm going!

How shall I get there? My contract with the car rental company is about to expire, and I return the car. It's not easy to say goodbye to a car you liked and got to know intimately, but this is part of life. Nothing lasts forever except, maybe, the Chinese.

I take a taxi to the Chinese.

•

The China Event takes place in a nice restaurant, with a bunch of Chinese and Germans.

There are speeches here, but I'm starving and I need to eat.

I take my seat at a table, where the following people sit: An atheist German, a religious German and two Chinese. The Atheist, a man, says that Germany must accept all refugees, with no limits. That's the ethical thing to do. The religious German, a young blonde lady, says that she is of two minds about the refugees, and confesses that "I don't feel good saying this, but when I walk on the street I'm afraid, especially when I see certain people walking by. I'm doubly careful."

What do you mean by "certain people"? Do you mean refugees?

"Yes."

The Chinese says: "In ten years this country will become Islamic."

What will you do when this happens?

"I'll move back to China."

Second Chinese says: "The reason why Germany allows so many refugees to come to this country is because of the Germans' guilty feelings about the Second World War."

I start eating.

Hello, Refugees!

I have no idea what food I'm eating but it's good, and that's good enough for me.

On the next day, I'm at the plaza outside Cologne's central train station, staring at the immense Gothic structure, known as Cologne Cathedral, right near me.

I take some moments to admire what I see and then go for coffee at Starbucks.

The Sylvester horror story that unfolded here, in the plaza and around it, took place months and months ago. Most likely not one of the many tourists visiting the Cathedral or sipping coffee at Starbucks was here on Sylvester night.

But there are some restaurants here, and I can try to have a little chat with a waiter or a waitress.

The first waitress I meet says that she left the area at 9:00 pm on Sylvester Eve, and she didn't see much, but she did notice that many "foreigners" were gathering in the plaza, some of whom bought drinks from her.

Are you talking about Arabs?

"Yes. Arabs and Africans."

I walk over to another eatery, Gaffel am Dom, which is pretty big. A waiter tells me that he was right here on Sylvester night.

What did you see? I ask him.

"Scheisse, that's what I saw."

Hello, Refugees!

What kind of Scheisse?

"I don't want to talk."

Other waitresses and waiters in this restaurant also refuse to talk. Why would you not talk? I ask one of them.

"We're not allowed."

Who said?

"The boss."

Why?

"Because the media came and asked questions and the boss said we are not allowed to talk."

Sounds like I'm in a really free country.

I've been to this place many times before. I like the Cathedral, and I like Cologne. But now the plaza looks somehow different. What's different? Many cops around. Is this police presence a result of what happened here on Sylvester? I ask a cop. Yes, it is, he says.

I stick around, looking for more witnesses, and I light up. I walk here and there, there and here in the plaza and when my cigarette is done I drop the butt and step on it.

The cop I talked with before walks over to me.

"What you just did," he admonishes me, "is against the law. That's €35 fine. I won't file a report this time, but if you do it again—"

These cops can't stop rapists, but they can stop smokers.

Who else could I ask what really happened here?

Years back I made my acquaintance with a lady who goes by the name of Barbara Schock-Werner. She used to be the Dombaumeisterin (master of cathedral architecture) of the Cologne Cathedral, and I remember her as a kind and brave human being. I wonder if she was here on Sylvester and so I dial the number I still have of her. She picks up, and we schmooze.

Yes, she says, she was in the Cathedral on Sylvester. Could we meet? I ask. Yes, she says. She happens to be not far from here, she tells me, and I invite her for coffee at Starbucks. Would she mind coming by? I ask her.

She would be glad to come by, but in thirty minutes from now.

And in exactly 30 minutes' time, on the dot, she shows up at Starbucks.

Don't you love Germany? On the dot, baby!

She speaks:

"I was in the Cathedral, for the Mass. Always at the end of the year, at 6:30 pm there's a Mass at the Cathedral. There was a Mass at this church (she points to a church to the right of us) also, at 6:00. A lot of people were in the plaza, even at 6:00, and they threw fireworks at both the Cathedral and the church. It was very horrible inside; it's horrible when you are in the church, and you hear the explosions."

Doesn't it happen every year?

"Yes, but not like this; this year there were many more fireworks. The police must have known that this year it was not normal."

What was not normal?

"People were aggressive; they wanted to smash the Cathedral. There were many people this year at such an early hour, earlier than other years. When we left the Cathedral, about eight o'clock, we couldn't pass through, because there were so many people here."

What kind of the people did you see here?

"People of color. Brown skin. And most of them were men."

So this is the way it went. Aggressive "brown" people throwing fireworks on churches and raping women. But the elite of Germany tried to cover it up because they don't want Frauke Petry and her friends to enter the Bundestag, come election time.

This is Germany, the Germany that wants Britain to stick around in the EU family.

Time passes, and the Brits vote on the referendum. They vote Leave, 52 to 48 percent. Germany is shocked. Europe is shocked.

Financial markets fall drastically.

Why did the Brits vote to leave? Here's how the *New York Times*, amongst many others, explains it: "Fear of being overrun by immigrants was a driving concern for 'Leave' voters."

To the British people, by the way, "immigrants" mean those from the Middle East as well as those from other European countries, such as Poland or Romania.

As for the refugees from the Middle East et al., the Europeans show them the way out without a referendum. This is from the BBC, fresh from the oven: "An agreement between Turkey and the European Union to halt migrants from traveling to Greek islands has reduced boat arrivals by 98% during the first five months of the year."

•

There are some Germans, admittedly quite a few, who do speak their minds in public. There are even a couple of German politicians on the center-left who don't shy away from saying what the politically correct tribe forbids. The Green Party mayor of Tübingen, Boris Palmer, is an example. Geographically speaking, Boris is 250 miles away from me, but I go to see him anyway. I board a train going to Stuttgart, get myself a 0.3-liter cup of coffee, and look at the German landscape unfolding in front of me.

In due time I meet His Honor in a café near Stuttgart. Boris orders coffee, I order Cola Light, and we chat.

Boris is a feisty guy, he's full of life, and he has a great figure. He is Green, how could he not?

If I have it right, I say to Boris, you are for setting limits on immigration. Is it correct?

"Yes."

And if I got it right, you also said that the use of weapons by soldiers at Germany's borders, to enforce those limits, was okay with you.

"Well, not the 'use' of weapons but to have soldiers carry weapons."

What will they do with the weapons?

"They don't have to use the weapons. To enforce the rules, it's enough to have soldiers on the border."

All carrying weapons?

"Yes, that's what soldiers do everywhere in the world."

And if people cross against the soldiers' orders, could the soldiers use their weapons?

"You don't have to shoot refugees. The Balkan states have stopped refugees from crossing their borders" without shooting at them.

You mean with tear gas?

"We are not in Gaza, are we?"

How the heck did Gaza sneak in here? I know that years ago Boris supported awarding the German Federal Cross of Merit to a staunch critic of Israel, the Jewish lawyer Felicia Langer, but who was talking about Gaza now? Perhaps this was a Freudian slip; he heard "Gaza" when I said "tear gas." I tell him that I said tear gas, not Gaza.

Is tear gas okay to be used against refugees?

Tear gas, he says, is no problem and it's even used "in German demonstrations."

Let me ask you a question. Let's say that there are soldiers on the border, and hundreds of thousands of refugees are trying to cross it, despite the tear gas. Can the soldiers shoot, let's say, in the air?

Boris refuses to answer this question. This question is hypothetical, he says, and he won't answer it.

The fact is that everything we are talking about at this café is hypothetical since the borders to Germany are closed anyway.

We talk a bit more and, of course, I can't resist asking this Gaza politician what I asked Volker, another Green: Europeans are flouting the Geneva Convention on Refugees, but at the same time they accuse Israel of violating the other Geneva Convention. Aren't they hypocritical?

"When you point a finger at the other, three fingers point back at you," he says.

Correct.

•

Some German companies, I've heard, don't have the time to point a finger at anybody because they are busy doing the good work. Daimler, for example. Daimler, I was told, is pouring massive amounts of money on refugees. Where does the money go? Into two lanes: Internships, through which refugees gain technical knowledge that will help them get jobs in other companies; and apprenticeships, where refugees are trained to actually work with the company.

Hello, Refugees!

Who's spreading these rumors? Daimler's press folks.

This is exciting news, and I ask to see the Daimler refugees at work.

Daimler says: Welcome!

Would be nice, don't you think, if I get to meet Ahmad from Hotel Wauer at a Daimler plant! What a picture that would be: Ahmad building the newest Mercedes and his hiding wife is out of her room, gracing the German landscape of humanity with her shining beauty.

That would be the day!

Chapter 24

Daimler Teaches a Refugee How to Screw

I am at Daimler's headquarter in Stuttgart, sitting with Wilfried Porth, Member of the Board of Daimler and the man in charge of Daimler's Human Resources.

I don't know the man, but I think he should be renamed King Wilfried.

Why do I think so?

Read the following four rules and you will agree.

First rule: When you are to meet King Wilfried, don't bother ordering a cab or driving yourself to His castle.

No.

Instead, be prepared for a new Mercedes to pick you up from wherever you are.

Second rule: When you come to visit King Wilfried, don't expect the King to be waiting for you downstairs. No, kings don't do that. Instead, you will have finely-dressed servants waiting to greet you, granting you a hot smile, and warmly asking you how you are doing. They will open the door for you; don't push any door. Once you are in the palace, another well-dressed servant will ask you how you are doing, offer you a lovely smile, and then walk with you to the King's Room.

Third rule: Once you are in the King's Room, don't expect the King to be there. Not yet, my dear.

Fourth rule: You'll be asked by great-looking Daimler employees, Would you like a drink?

Cola Light with ice, I say.

Oh God in Heaven! I am probably the first breathing soul who utters such a low-class request inside this palace since, at least, 1945.

But this is Daimler, and Daimler got a Coke.

Daimler got everything, in case you ever doubted it.

It is at this sensitive moment that His Honor, dressed in a polo shirt, enters.

Hello, Refugees!

I can't believe that King Wilfried Porth the First is wearing a polo shirt!

The King and I chat about everything, but nothing with which I'm familiar. I want the King to tell me one thing: Could Your Greatness, please, describe a Mercedes car in a poetic way?

The King has no fucking clue what I want from his life. He can give me specs, he can give me speeds, he can give me strengths, horses and powers, but he can't, for the life of him, describe Mercedes in a poetic way.

Literature, I beg of my King, the King of all Kings. Give me a line, my Lord, a literary line that would paint for me a Mercedes car. Bitte!

The King can not.

His press people in the room can't come up with one-quarter of a poetic line that would describe even the costliest Mercedes.

The King then talks about human resources, refugee interns and refugee apprentices.

Only that these concepts are too theoretical for me. I would like to see the interns, to chat with the apprentices, to shake hands with the Daimler refugees. Could this be arranged?

Of course. Everything one ever wanted can be given him by Daimler. Daimler, didn't you know, is the fulfiller of all human wishes.

An elegantly dressed pressperson is at the ready to drive me to a Mercedes-Benz plant.

Fantastic!

The drive is enjoyable, in a Mercedes of course, and before I know it we have arrived at the location of my wish. Welcome to the Mercedes-Benz plant in Sindelfingen. This is not a factory, my friend; this is a city!

In case you like numbers: there are 35,000 people working here.

It is here, my dear, where they manufacture the S-Class.

Look at that S! That's a car!

Most of the people buying this car, I'm told, are CEOs and other rare creatures, and for the most part, they don't drive it. Who drives the S-Class? Personal drivers.

If I owned this S, I wouldn't let anybody touch it!

But before we move forward here, my dearest, let me share one more detail with you. The figure of 35,000 people does not include a group of journalists who are here for the purpose of seeing the Daimler refugee workers.

How do I know?

The plant's press people are joining us, and they have a number of journalists with them. One of the journalists tells me that she's from New York, working for Bloomberg News; the rest are locals.

The Daimler's folks must be preparing a special exhibition for us, maybe a whole floor of refugees working on the classy Class.

I can't wait!

We are being led to another floor and gently walk between sophisticated robots, as we advance toward the refugee engineers, refugee interns and refugee apprentices of Daimler.

Stop!

Here is the first refugee on the floor.

His name, so he says, is Adham and he is 26 years of age. He arrived in Germany in January 2014 and now he is an intern here.

Adhan is acquiring technical knowledge that will prepare him for his next job.

In seconds he is going to show us what he has learned thanks to Daimler's generosity.

Hello, Refugees!

Technical knowledge at a Mercedes plant is undoubtedly complex and I can hardly contain my excitement. It's not every day that I get to see a Syrian refugee on his way to the highest of the tech and car industry in this rich country of Germany.

The moment is coming, my dear! Adhan is about to demonstrate to us his technical knowhow and acumen.

Oh Lordy Lord!

Watch, my dears, what Adhan is doing right now: Adhan screws the three-pointed star to the car hood.

Yeah!

This operation, the art of screwing, takes him two seconds.

Ja!

And he does it again and again; this is an assembly line, after all.

Yeah. Adham was taught how to screw.

I don't know if I should cry or weep.

Not knowing what to do, I approach Adhan in Arabic, in the hope that Daimler press people don't know the language.

I ask him to share his life dream with me.

You wouldn't guess it in a thousand years, but this is his dream: To marry a blonde girl.

And now, you tell me: Is there a blonde girl in Germany who wouldn't excitedly run to the wedding bed of an Arab who can screw a three-pointed star?

So, this was Adham.

Where are the other refugees?

Not here, my friend.

We are done with refugees for this floor.

Of course, Adhan is not the only refugee we are about to see and meet today.

Next, we go to see Hassan.

Hassan does office work, don't ask me what exactly, and he poses for a picture.

The journalists, all equipped with cameras, take photos of Hassan, but not before they make sure that he has his right fingers on the mouse and his left fingers on the keyboard.

They click, click, click and click their cameras.

Hello, Refugees!

This is an awesome image, isn't it? Hassan, the refugee, can put fingers on a mouse and on a keyboard at the very same moment!

That's multitasking, isn't it!

I used to have a cat that did it: one paw on the mouse and one paw on the keyboard – and she was three months old. But who could ever believe that Hassan, a Hassan, could do this as well?

Take a pic! Another one! Another one! Another one!

These are the same journalists, don't you ever forget, who explain Brexit to you. They are also the ones who will tell you that it's okay to bully Akif if you happen to meet him on the street.

Adham and Hassan, as you can tell, are the first refugees we get to meet at this plant.

They are also the last ones. Yes.

What a blessed man I am! I got to meet two refugee queers at a Green Party event and two Arabs at a Mercedes plant. Could life be more exciting?

Hello, Refugees!

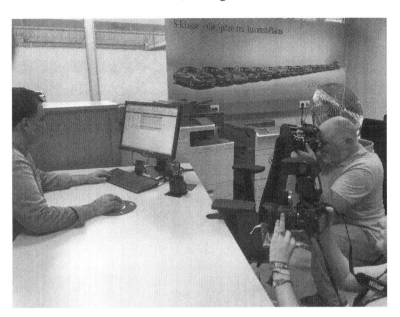

Chapter 25

We Need a Private Home, For Free, Plus Monthly Stipends,
Free Health Insurance, and Free Education

Yes, life can be more exciting; believe it or not.

Meet, my dear, Jürgen Todenhöfer. Have you heard of him? A gazillion Germans have. Jürgen is a businessman who for some years served as Vice Chairman on the Board of Hubert Burda Media, a multi-billion-dollar company. Jürgen was also a politician, serving as a member of the Bundestag from 1972 to 1990. In addition to all the above, the man is an author, a journalist, and an activist. His biggest claim to fame, hear this, came about in 2014 when he became "the first western journalist allowed to enter ISIS-controlled Syria and Iraq – and to return safely," in the words of the *Guardian*.

Why did he go there? Well, because the man thinks big of himself. What does he think of himself? He sees himself as "Germany's most renown Middle East and anti-terror expert as well as strong critic of the US-led war on terror."

How do I know? This is what I was told by his office, in response to an email to him.

How humble.

During the years, Jürgen has made it quite clear to all who wanted to know that he is a person in love with the Muslim world and with the Quran as well. Jürgen, as you might expect, has strong opinions about Israel and the Palestinians, championing the Palestinian cause, but I want to hear what he thinks about the refugee issue.

And so, on this very day, we meet at Café Einstein on Unter den Linden, the same place where I met Gregor Gysi.

Remember that adorable man?

Jürgen is not Gregor. Gregor has charm, Jürgen does not. Jürgen is so narcissistic, let me tell you, that no charm can penetrate his persona. What saves him, though, is his excellent sense of humor. I have a very good time with him, and we laugh a lot while together.

But it's time to talk about serious stuff: refugees.

Give me an overview of the refugee story in Germany, I ask him.

"How many hours do you give me?"

Until they close the café.

"We are all refugees. We all come from Africa. Then we went to the Middle East, and from the Middle East we came to Europe. So essentially, even the Germans are African. This is something that people forget!"

Here I obviously have another Christian Springer.

What's the story with the refugees now in Germany? So far Germany has allowed in more refugees than any other European country. Why? I ask the man.

"This question you have to ask our Chancellor, Angela Merkel, because she decided to open our borders, almost without any restriction." But it's not only Angela, he adds. "The majority of Germans supported this policy. I think that one day the Germans will be proud of what we call 'Welcoming culture,' the way that we have received the refugees."

Other European countries haven't done this. Why are the Germans so much kinder, so much nicer, so much lovelier than the rest of the Europeans?

"Early on there were right-wing protests (against having refugees in Germany)—"

You mean, Pegida?

"And we wanted to show that they don't command the discussion about refugees."

To show whom?

"Us."

Are you telling me that the Germans accepted over a million refugees because the Germans wanted to show Mr. Lutz Bachmann that he's wrong?

"We wanted to do the right thing. We wanted to show that Mr. Bachmann and Pegida did not speak for the German population."

Are the Germans so fucked up that they bring in a millions refugees just to show Lutz Bachmann that he's an idiot?

187

Hello, Refugees!

"The right-wing used words such as 'Dirty Arab' and 'raping refugees' when describing the refugees, and we wanted to show that those words were not said in our name."

There are anti-immigrant parties in other European countries, and their members describe refugees in similar manners, but none of those countries welcomed a million refugees in response. Why is that?

"They don't have our history." German anti-immigrants, he adds, "repeat words that the Nazis used against Jews when they talk about Muslims, Arabs and black people."

Hey, Lutz: Did you hear? You are more powerful than Mama! You thought Mama was powerful, forget it! Mama is full of fears, my man! Look what you have done with your truck and your nuts: You brought in over a million refugees to Germany, and many more are to come every year from now on. You are stronger than that man of eighty years ago, Führer Lutz!

Jürgen and I keep talking, and he tells me that having immigrants in this country is a blessing. "Since 1970 the Germans reproduce themselves only by sixty-five percent. This means that in 2050 the number of people over sixty-five will double, and the number of working people will be going down. We urgently need immigrants, at least 800,000 every year. But we need to choose the people, the right people."

I leave Jürgen, and in just a few days I find out, with millions of Germans, that the Refugee Blessing might very soon rise to an Infinite Blessing before we know it.

Something happened, and Germany's Infinite Blessing is slowly becoming a horror story of immense proportions. Millions of dark-skinned people, pay attention to this, could soon pop out in private homes through the toilet pipes – to use Springer's lively imagery.

Yeah.

What happened? Something big!

Yeah. Something big happened while Mama and the rest of us were not paying attention, but once we realize what's cooking in the world's kitchen behind our back, we are totally shocked.

What happened is this: Papa Recep was having a good time away from his palace when a bunch of Turks started a coup.

Will the junta keep the deal with Mama?, asks every German with a reasonable IQ.

Nobody can tell. The only thing left to do is what every European leader worth more than one penny does. Without the tiniest hesitation, they shout out of every window of the European Continent: Keep Democracy Alive, No to military coups!

Their wish comes true in less than a day and Papa Recep, the biggest Democrat of our time, easily squashes the coup. To keep democracy alive and booming in Turkey, here are some of the initial steps Papa takes, as reported by the BBC: "More than 50,000 people have been rounded up, sacked or suspended from their jobs by Turkey's government in the wake of last week's failed coup. The purge of those deemed disloyal to President Recep Tayyip Erdogan widened on Tuesday to include teachers, university deans and the media."

Merciful Papa also shows an interest in reinstituting the death penalty in his country. There's no better democratic visual, you must admit, than that of thousands of people falling to the ground at the very same moment by a long line of free-thinking shooting squads.

Ja.

Life is good. Everything is good. Germany is saved.

And while every German must be happy, drinking a beer or five in honor of Papa, I have nothing better to do than wonder: How are Tanios and Maha, my first refugees, doing? Are they still up north in Hamburg's villa neighborhood of Harvestehude?

I'm in Hamburg now. Did I not mention it? Sorry.

I needed the company of northern Germans, to cool off my excitement. Happens to you too, on occasions, doesn't it?

In any case, I go to that refugee home in the nice villa neighborhood and, yes, T&M are still there.

How long have you been in this place? I ask them.

"Eight months," they say.

And today, unlike last time, their children are with them.

The children have their own room, of course, but everybody is in the parents' room now, getting ready to eat dinner together.

There goes my coffee, I'm afraid; for there will be no coffee for a while.

The older son, sixteen years of age, is "very good in mathematics," Tanios tells me.

Why did you leave Lebanon? I ask the genius son.

"I don't know," he answers. He didn't want to leave, he tells me. He wanted to stay in Lebanon together with his friends, but the parents took him with them to Germany. "I cried a lot when they told me that we were leaving."

Tanios shows me the German language exam that he took recently. His score is 53, and he is very proud of it. I want to ask him if he knows how to say "I peel potatoes," but before I have a chance to say anything the man interrupts my thoughts. "Will you help us?" he asks. "We want to get a private home." He suggests that I talk to some people, other Germans like me, who will find a good place for them.

Yeah.

Hello, Refugees!

Well, I'm writing it right here; if you want to buy them a home, preferably one newly built, be my guest.

Never again, Maha tells me, will she go back to Lebanon. Germany is good, Germany's the best, and the Germans love the Lebanese. Everything's free here, the children get a good education, which is also free, and all that's missing in life is a private home, a villa.

Chapter 26

Adios, Germany

I miss the Mahane Yehuda market in Jerusalem. There they have good coffee, as good as Tanios', and excellent goat cheeses, as excellent as Götz's.

Yes, I know: In Mahane Yehudah I won't find Gregor Gysi's breakfasts and in Jerusalem I won't find transgender Afghanis, Majdal Shams refugees, Daimler Syrians who can screw, and no Thawanni will be walking the streets of the Holy City.

But I need a break. I need a break from the Good Germans. After years of being told that they were bad, they cherish their newly-found good reputation, but are they really good? Sneak into the camps, and see for yourself. Watch the decay, smell the stench, feel the mixing together of enemies, eat the food and be a witness to the rest the of the miserable conditions that refugees must contend with every hour of every day of every month. The only thing that functions in this whole "Refugees Welcome" p.r. is what worked so well last century: perfect transport organization. Refugees are transported into camps and homes all over the country in the most efficient way imaginable. Every refugee is shipped to an exact location on the exact minute, all in perfect order. Amazingly, none of the Good People has spent one second asking themselves: What next? What are we going to do with this million once we've transported them?

Yes, I know: the idea is that one day these people will live in their private dwellings, and perhaps by the time this book comes out – two years after Merkel's "We can do it" – some of the refugee camps mentioned in this book will no longer be. But the horrifying months and years that the refugees have spent in the atrocious camps will surely make their mark. The psychological, mental and spiritual damage incurred will almost certainly haunt them and those around them, and the German society as a whole, for generations to come.

Hello, Refugees!

The Germans fight one another about the refugee issue but, honestly, I didn't find any difference between the Germans on the right and the Germans on the left, between them who demonstrate against refugees and them who hang the largest "Refugees Welcome" posters on the tallest of trees, all the while that they enjoy Mama's deal with Turkey. Both sides, right and left, care about the refugees as much as I care about King Ludwig II.

Not that I've fallen head over heels with the refugees. I love the Arab culture but I know it well enough to understand that not all I'm told is true. Lying in the Middle Eastern world, where my soul resides, shares not much in common with lying in the Western world. In the Middle East, often enough, "lying" is the sibling of storytelling, and is equally cherished. It's a game, the game of life. But, visiting the camps, I didn't have to rely on stories; I saw much with my own eyes.

I need a cigarette, an Indonesian cigarette.

Oops. I can't get them. In every tobacco shop I visit, I hear the same song: "We don't carry clove cigarettes anymore." Why not? "It's against the law." What happened? It turns out that my Indonesian cigarettes, due to some EU law, are no longer legal in this land. I can't find one tobacco shop that sells them. This is Germany, where the 5.8-meter rule is taken extremely serious.

I get myself a plane ticket to the Holy Land, where the Jews train the Daesh fighters.

Once there, I'll get myself a cup of boiling Arabic coffee, with no 0.3 marks, or an ice-cold Diet Coke, sit on a bench and slowly sip my drink, while constantly turning my head right and left to make sure nobody is about to stab me. Yeah, this is one of those rituals you better observe in the Holy City nowadays. In Israel they might not have Syrians, but they have Palestinians – some of whom are in love with the knife.

And late at night, when the shops of Mahane Yehudah Market close, the bars and restaurants open, and all over you see people drinking, eating and dancing.

I need it.

Once away from this country, I know that in a matter of days I'll miss it.

I'll miss the Arabs. I'll miss Kossai, I'll miss Suleiman and the rest of Akko, I'll miss the Arab potato peelers, and I'll miss lovely Thawanni.

And yes, I'll miss the Germans. After everything is said and done, I must admit that I love them. Don't ask me why. It is the fate of the Jew, don't you know, to love those who hate him.

Auf Wiedersehen.

End

Tuvia Tenenebom

Hamburg

©2017

Made in the USA
Middletown, DE
26 March 2018